I Can't Wear Wool

Kim Märkl

For Key, Raphael, and Raimati

Contents

Follow Me

When I joined the three billion users on Facebook, I felt like an outsider crashing a party in full swing, a middle-aged wallflower lost in a prodigious outpouring of autobiographical material, and a loner traversing an unfamiliar landscape.

Friends are the hood ornament of every social media profile. With that in mind, I uploaded a buffet of data for the ads algorithm, then searched for playmates in the world's largest playground. Friend bingers paraded hundreds, even thousands of friends, and users with a low friend count presumably forfeited friendships with strangers. Facebook was as bewildering as my wedding; family, friends, acquaintances, and people I had never met, all hanging out in one place. An abundance of real-life friends would exhaust me and paralyze my life, but digital pals en masse, why not? Amazingly, moments after establishing my account, Facebook sent a list of people I might know. Big Brother was right on the money, and I had a friend count within minutes. Though I prefer the term pen pals since I've never met a good number of them.

After several weeks of regular visits to the platform, I realized that Facebook adores record keeping. There's a good chance they have one of the most extensive libraries on the planet. Every post, comment, like, follow, and share is archived. At the end of the day, you can delete the jellied moose nose recipe from your page, but just because you can't see it doesn't mean it's gone. So, think twice before posting. We've given social media a terrifying amount of power, and they aren't wearing halos.

Facebook, the world's ultimate stage, is humming with comedy, absurdity, romance, and tragedy twenty-four hours a day. Mark's creation brings out the best and worst in us. Had the Bard (what a great username) had access to social media, he may have posted, "All the world's on Facebook and all the men and women merely players; they have their exits and their entrances, their posts, and their comments, and one man in his time plays many parts." Big like for you, Will.

The nuances of human emotion are enthusiastically expressed through emojis. The most popular icons include the heart, thumbs up, and four disembodied heads. Emojis are gifts and make no mistake, this show of solidarity is reciprocal. Moreover, there's no better way to vitalize a relationship than with an ego-boosting like. And let's face it, if you want to be liked, you too must click like. Fortunately, Facebook cannot discern the genuine from the perfunctory like.

One day, I noticed my son was not reciprocating my likes, so I called him.

"Why don't you like my posts?"

"Because I never like anything on Facebook."

"But I'm your mother. I made you, can't you like me?"

"Sorry, I never click like. I just don't."

"You are forsaking all conventional social media behavior. Then again, you never have to pretend to like something you don't."

"That's right."

Negative and venomous comments are on my no-go list. Politics is also an uncontrollable demon and is best avoided. Not to mention, conflicting political views make people not like each other. Political posts, like volatile oil, catch fire quickly, spread out of control, and leave a trail of smoldering ashes in their wake.

Relationships can be polished or tarnished on Facebook, and that's why I hide offensive posts. Who needs more contention in their life. Blips and bleeps announcing updates, a new profile picture, or the end of the world disrupt my day; therefore my phone thwarts them.

Since surfing on my mobile is about as comfortable as wearing thong underwear, I log into Facebook from a dated iMac. Usually, this ritual occurs in the evening, accompanied by a glass of wine. Also, I never frolic for more than five or ten minutes. My news feed flashes onto the screen, and images of cherubic offspring prettify the landscape. Ads for the frying pan I recently ordered on Amazon are nestled between an adorable puppy and vacation photos. The puppy has many admirers and receives oodles of hearts and smiley faces, which obviously delights the owner because he thanks his audience with an abundance of warm and fuzzy symbols. Naturally, I give the puppy a thumbs up. Another friend discloses his worldview, and an irritated user rejects it. A heated debate follows. Regardless, I have moved on to an amusing video of a chicken running ecstatically into the arms of its owner. Occasionally, I rant at the screen, and once in a while, I post something that is not particularly revealing. One evening, inspired by Warhol, I was tempted to post a picture of a box of frozen spinach, but my courage failed me.

Over time, Facebook lost its allure, so I decided to say goodbye. The algorithm interrupted the process and asked, "Are you sure you want to break up? Why don't you deactivate your account and put it in the attic for a while? You may return one day."

"That seems like an attractive solution. Now, hold on a second, you're manipulating me. I'm deleting my account and scattering its binary remains in cyberspace."

"Your loss, loser, I mean, user."

Doorbell Lady

Jogging with our King Charles Spaniel, affectionately known as Beethoven, is exhausting. His leash is wrapped around my right hand, which prevents me from swinging my arms and impedes the rhythm of running. Not only that, the animal yanks my arm every time he lurches, which is often. Sure, I could jog alone, come home, harness the dog, and lope around again. Or I could call my pet products sales rep brother for advice. After listening to me whine, he says, "You need a dog-jog belt. It's a great gimmick. The hands-free leash attaches to a belt around your waist. I'll send you one."

The package arrived, and I tethered our high-strung sixteen-pound pet to my torso. I am woefully slower than this canine classified a toy by the Kennel Club, and feel like a large bouncy parasite chasing its host as we barrel down the road. Frankly, his strength is a mystery to me, given that he has four carrot-like limbs jutting from his tiny body and is endowed with more fur than muscles. Should you happen to see us, you would think his name is Bubbles or Peanut. Just imagine his mother's womb, twenty-four unwieldy legs poking that poor bitch in the ribs. Thank dog gestation is merely two months.

After we get to the woods, I cut the rope, and the animal zigzags around the forest. His neurotransmitters must be playing pinball in the olfactory region of his brain because bells ring with each whiff of enticing excrement and pee-pee. According to my husband, he's reading the newspaper. Once, the dog ran into the adjoining field, picked up a tractor-flattened field mouse, and pranced around with his trophy, pretending to be a hunter. What's next, big boy? Are you going to bring Mommy a garden gnome?

One day, I was running with the dog when an old woman stepped out of her front gate, waved me down, and said something incomprehensible. I wondered whether she needed medical assistance, so I crossed the road, straining to hear her. Her plea for help flicked on the dog's barking switch, and it's anyone's guess how to turn it off. After ten years, we still haven't found the mute button.

"I'm waiting for a delivery, and my doorbell is broken," she said fretfully.

"Sorry, but I don't know anything about doorbells. I'll send my husband over when he gets home from work."

"I can't wait. The delivery man is coming this afternoon."

"I'm not sure how I can help."

The yapping escalated, and the frenetic animal danced in erratic circles around my legs, yet Doorbell Lady seemed unaware of my predicament.

"Can you have a look at it?" she pleaded.

"I guess so. Although looking is not the same as fixing."

Reluctantly, I followed the woman up the front path to her tidy home. I was already apprehensive about repairing the bell, but how could I accomplish the task with a neurotic animal affixed to me?

Once inside, the wound-up pooch yanked me in every direction and completely ignored my sit, stay, no, and down commands. I was more uptight than my mother when she ran out of cigarettes. In any case, Doorbell Lady's helplessness had a firm grip on me. Maybe we're hardwired for altruism, even when there's nothing we can do to help.

The old woman pointed to a doorbell mounted near the ceiling. Despite my trepidation, I asked for a stepladder and a screwdriver. Surprisingly, she brought me a chair ideally suited to the job. Then again, how I could examine the doorbell, I wondered, without strangling our simple-minded pet? I wrestled with the yellowed plastic cover and felt relieved when it came off without cracking. Inside was a little silver bell and an enormous square battery, so either the battery or the wiring leading to the outdoor button was on the fritz.

With my newfound voice of authority, I asked the woman whether she had a replacement battery. She rummaged through her junk drawer. Most of the batteries in our junk drawer are dead, yet this woman presented me with a brand-new package of C cells. I disconnected the square power cell and handed it to her. "This is what you need. I'll take it with me and pick one up, but it won't be here in time for your delivery."

"Just a minute, my son recently bought an extra battery."

She went into another room and returned with the correct power cell. While I replaced the battery, Beethoven thought it might be fun to howl.

"Let's see if it works," I said.

The lady stepped outside and pushed the button. Fancy that, the bell tolled. But for whom, oh yeah, the delivery guy.

"Glad to be of help," I said, shaking her hand.

We sprinted home, and the worn-out dog turned in circles before curling himself into a doughnut on the kitchen floor. You'd think that dogs would have kicked the bed-building habit after twelve thousand years of domestication, especially when napping on ceramic tiles.

Without the dog underfoot, I loaded boxes into the car for a trip to the donation center. Doorbell Lady was on my mind as I pressed the close button on the garage door remote. Alas, the trunk was open, and the sound of the door crushing our car's yawning hatchback turned my stomach. Frantically, I pushed another button, and the door squealed to a halt, fusing the trunk lid to the garage door. Afraid of causing further damage, I waited for my husband to return.

When Key got home, he put the car in gear, pushed it forward a few inches, and released them from their steely embrace. Fortunately for us, we drive an old, banged-up Corolla, and at some point in the life of a car, you say, one more dent, so what. Come to think of it, that's how I feel about myself.

I can only say this: my good deed did not protect me from misfortune, so I have never jogged down that street again.

Wedding

The wedding whisperer entered the kitchen carrying her clipboard, then sat down at the table and declared, "I have been dreaming of your wedding since the day you were born." That decree safeguarded my mother's position as the master of ceremonies and fulfilled her unbending need to run the show. I looked up from the comic section of the newspaper and blinked. Honestly, my mother was not infringing on my dream because I never had a wedding fantasy. All the same, I yearned for a low-key event.

"Mom, why don't we have a subdued ceremony followed by lunch with a few guests at a local restaurant?" My proposal was pooh-poohed because it was god-awful. Instead, my creator craved an elaborate sit-down dinner at a venue with a dance floor. This wedding was her epic poem, and from her pen flowed dresses, bouquets, menus, and limos.

I looked at my mother, knowing very well that she would pretend to consider my ideas and then use her decades-old dream to legitimize her inherent right to take charge. She unclamped several sheets of paper from her clipboard and handed them to me. "Do you want to have a look at the guest list?" At least she packaged it as a rhetorical question. I skimmed the names and sighed.

"Mom, Key, and I don't know many of these people. Who are they?"

"Our friends! They would be terribly hurt if we did not invite them."

Frantically, I pointed at more unfamiliar names.

"And who are they?"

"Those are your father's colleagues, and he wants them to be present. In fact, it means a lot to him."

"Are you sure about that? Does Dad even like them?"

"Yes, he does. We have attended several of their children's weddings and given generous gifts. It would be embarrassing if we did not invite them." And there it was, the crux of the issue; gifts are reciprocal. To give is to get. Even better is to give a discounted item and receive a full-priced one in return.

She turned back to her clipboard and sighed.

"Have you chosen your bridesmaids?"

"My sister will be my bridesmaid, and Key's brother will be his best man."

She had to nibble on this before consenting. A large procession was undoubtedly parading down the aisle of her dream, yet she pacified me and didn't kick up a fuss. Huh, no fire-works today?

"What will your sister wear as the lone bridesmaid?"

Her inquiry rode on a wisp of sarcasm.

"She could wear one of her old prom dresses. In fact, she can wear whatever she wants."

My mother mentally browsed the dress rack in the attic.

"Let me think about it."

Ho, ho, ho, that is simply not true. You will not think about it. Instead, you will pick up the phone and spend hours contemplating the dress situation with your sisters. No guidelines existed for a pre-worn bridesmaid's dress, and all the nuances had to be clarified. They would chew the cud on this one.

"Have you thought about your bridal gown? I know this wonderful little boutique in Pennsylvania."

"I thought I could wear your wedding dress, Mom?"

"Oh yes," she said, smiling, "I would like that very much." We genuinely connected with the dress.

"My veil is in bad shape, so we definitely need to get a new one," she said.

I knew that opposing the veil was pointless. Had I, for one moment, contemplated walking down the aisle unveiled, she would have said to herself, my daughter is bonkers, to use one of her favorite words. Ironically, individualism is a defining trait of Western culture, while conformity is the soup du jour when it comes to weddings. Across the globe, brides are exchanging their colorful wedding attire for our white matrimonial uniform.

"Let's discuss the music for the reception. Do you have a band in mind?"

"We don't want a band. Key and I would prefer a quiet wedding."

"You're not going to have a wedding without dancing, are you?" And there it was, her signature move, a statement disguised as a question.

"Mom, my future husband can't dance, and I'm not crazy about it either. Plus, bands are loud. So think about it, after they crank up all that sound equipment, I won't be able to hear what the strangers at my wedding are saying to me."

"Stop being facetious. Since you were born, I have imagined you dancing at your wedding. I have never been to a wedding without music."

I had no choice; the bridesmaid's dress was up for grabs, but not the band. I conceded.

"Colozza's Bakery will make the cake," she said matter-of-factly.

"Yup, that's great. You can have your cake and eat it too."

"Are you making fun?"

"I'm having fun. What's next?"

"We need a photographer. Mrs. Brown knows a good one. I'll speak to her."

"We would rather use a photography student and make the album ourselves. A professionally bound book is not really important to us."

There was only a slight frown of displeasure at my suggestion.

"I will give it some thought," she said.

Actually, our peaceful trade-offs and placatory approach made for a tolerable game of wedding tennis. With each volley, clenched teeth and derogatory comments were avoided.

"What about the rehearsal dinner?"

"I don't think we need a rehearsal dinner. Who would come anyway?"

"All the out-of-town people and the wedding party, of course."

"There are only two people in the wedding party. It would mean planning another event on top of creating an additional expense. All of this is adding up."

"We cannot have a rehearsal without a rehearsal dinner. It's a tradition!"

If you are familiar with the musical *Fiddler on the Roof*, feel free to sing or howl the word tradition. It appears that the Catholic families of Parma are just as devoted to traditions, especially regarding nuptials, as the Jewish community of Anatevka.

"I'd like to have wine and cheese on the patio. Dinner at a restaurant will cost a fortune."

"Then we'll have a pig roast. The pig roast company will provide the food and set everything up. We won't have to do anything."

"But they will not clean up. It is August in Cleveland, and it is sweltering. Do we want to roast a pig in 95-degree heat?"

"Yes, we do."

"Are we finished?"

"Not by a long shot. Our next order of business is choosing the flowers. Have you thought about what you want for the church and the tables at the reception?"

"No, the need for flowers never occurred to me."

"We must select bouquets for you and your sister and corsages for the best man, mother of the bride, mother of the groom, father of the bride, and father of the groom."

"Can't I carry a little bunch of wildflowers? I love wildflowers. Aren't corsages a bit old-fashioned?"

"Mea culpa, mea maxima culpa," she looked at the ceiling and cried with a dramatic beating of the breast.

I raised my eyebrows and simply agreed. Without exception, mea culpas closed the door to an argument.

"We still need to discuss the menu and your hair. You must have it done at the salon. I recommend a manicure as well."

"I have short nails, remember? So, if I polish my stubby Polish nails, it will only draw attention to their stubbiness. Don't you think?"

She ignored me and continued.

"Then there's the limo rental. Don't look at me like that; you are arriving in a limo, and your father is wearing a tux. Are you rolling your eyes? Yes, he's wearing a tux."

That night, after everyone had gone to bed, I uncorked a bottle of Cabernet and reflected on the day's events. The fact is, the marriage is yours. The wedding, however, belongs to your mother.

Kitchen Timer

This morning, my kitchen timer ticked until three minutes before the designated ring time, then petered out. I bought it a few years ago at a local kitchen store, a venue that managed to survive the online exodus, and headed back there to get a replacement. It is 2020, and we are in the midst of the Corona pandemic. Brick-and-mortar shopping has become an exercise in misery. The kitchen store is small, and only a handful of people are permitted inside at any given time. Every customer is required to take a basket at the store's entrance, and once the baskets are gone, the shop has reached its capacity. The rest of us must wait outside on strips of tape spaced six feet apart. Apparently, the airborne droplets we expel from our mouths and noses do not travel beyond the taped boundaries.

When it's my turn to enter the building, I pull a surgical face mask from my pocket and hook it behind my ears. I've been using the same mask for weeks and feel like I'm wearing an old Kleenex. I don't think I would use a tissue after it fell on the ground, yet I'm still wearing that mask. We have no choice in the matter, no mask, no service. As I exhale, warm air escapes through the top of the mask and fogs up my glasses. Since I can't hold my breath for the time it will take to buy the timer, the spectacles must come off, making my once foggy world fuzzy. Nearsightedness forces me to put my face close to the objects in the shop that interest me, and very quietly, my husband says, "People are gawking at you."

"I'm merely trying to see the timer, not smell it."

By the time I leave the store, I have accomplished nothing. The mask made me irritable, and there were no timers that I liked. Going out has lost its allure, so I go online instead and resentfully fund Bezos' plans to frolic in outer space. And yes, I admit to having a double standard; the online behemoth both annoys and pleases me.

The timer page is filled with an impressive array of options. A few of the digital timers have more features than my first computer. One timer is determined to make me a grill pro; never again will I cook a steak by *eye vision*. Astonishingly, that gadget will let me know whether my steak is rare, medium, or well done, and its lengthy instruction manual rendered by Google Translate is sure to entertain me. Instruction booklets for several household appliances have given me insight into Chinese syntax. For example, my eye massager promises to *resolve the pore bulky and eye bags problem, and the blu-ray function open, massage the eye can feel a little blue, at the same time your mood will become pleasant.* In other words, I will be a poreless, bagless, blue-eyed wonder in a fine mood after using this device.

Mechanical timers appeal to me more than digital devices. The good news is that dozens are available for less than ten dollars. As I scroll down the page, a droopy-eyed penguin timer catches my eye. It looks like a yellow-beaked Darth Vader and comes with an instructional video, just in case turning the dial clockwise, then counterclockwise, is not adequately explained in the instruction manual.

Nearly two thousand people took the time to review the penguin. According to one review, this adorable penguin can double as countertop décor. The customer must have been from France because she wrote it with the accent mark above the é. It's nice to know that the little penguin keeps entrées from burning. One penguin timer enthusiast highly recommended the little guy. Another devotee kept their toddler on schedule with it. I wish I had known that keeping a two-year-old on schedule simply required a penguin timer. Unfortunately, this wisdom comes about twenty-five years too late.

It turns out that Mr. Penguin has a flaw after all. He isn't precise when measuring short increments of time. Is that like saying the hour hand on my watch is accurate, but the minute hand isn't?

Several reviews mentioned the penguin was adorable and super cute but didn't ring. The words adorable and cute appeared so often I wondered whether most of the reviews were written by the same person.

At one point, I became completely absorbed reading the thoughts of strangers and forgot to continue my search for a timer. Suddenly, I found myself sitting in the kitchens of the world, drinking a cup of coffee and listening to the pros and cons of the penguin timer. For instance, one woman's vintage oven got really hot, and the back of her stove melted her poor plastic tomato timer. So, she wisely suggested not putting the poor little penguin next to a heat source, you guessed it, to prevent it from getting too hot. Julie thought the penguin was totally cute, but he didn't fulfill her needs. Brenda couldn't hear the bing over the sound of the shower. I was startled to read that Brenda timed her showers. Nevertheless, my favorite review said, "This timer was a waste of time."

The penguin was also evaluated for its ability to assist in potty training, yet received only two and a half stars for this feature. What if your child's creation is well underway when it rings? Do you lift him from the toilet seat and tell him his time is up? Wouldn't a ticking penguin add unnecessary stress to going potty? The timer received three and a half stars for easy to use but got four stars for giftable. If it's not easy to use and only works occasionally, and I can't use it for potty training, why would I give it to anybody? Because it's adorable, I guess.

Subway Mutiny

Even though I know better, I have expectations when traveling by train. I expect passengers to stare out the window or occupy themselves with inaudible devices. I've diagnosed myself with misophonia, a disorder that causes me to be oversensitive to noise. Not only do din and decibels get a rise out of me. I actually suffer genuine mental anguish. Evidence confirming my condition is abundant. For openers, I've asked waiters to turn down and even turn off the music in restaurants. Sure, my success rate is low, but there's no harm in trying. And seeing as my eye doctor replaced his waiting room magazines with a television, I no longer wish to wait there. The magazines were satisfying in a white cheddar popcorn kind of way, whereas the TV makes me want to stuff chewing gum in my ears. Phobias seize a person's rationality. Believe me, I have told myself repeatedly, *you will not be irked by noise.* I might as well try to control the weather through telepathy.

Usually, the perks of traveling by subway are substantial. Instead of navigating congested roads and hunting for a parking spot, I can savor forty-five minutes of uninterrupted reading. Yet, it is impossible for me to read while passengers are streaming loud music, and their earbuds don't muffle the noise. The fireworks emanating from headphones make me yearn to sever the umbilical cord connecting listeners to their devices.

Listening to Mozart supposedly increases intelligence, but have you ever heard Mozart leaking from a person's headphones? For the most part, I hear a high-strung mouse walloping a pair of cymbals. And what about the awesome adolescent blasting music from his mobile like a twentieth-century boom box? You know, if I were young and had the eyelashes of a giraffe, I might flirt him into submission. And there is nothing worse than being forced to listen to a loud, intimate phone conversation. One day, the purse across from me began mewing. The sound crescendoed to meowing, and before long, the bag was yowling. Catwoman rummaged frantically for her phone before pulling it out like a prize trout. Then she groaned about her failing health for the remainder of the ride.

After disembarking, my first thought is that I'd like to purchase some cannabis for the ride home. The problem is, I have no idea where to get it.

As soon as I board a train, I search for individuals who are reading, not swiping or typing. It baffles me why some people think texting should sound like a vintage typewriter. Silence is the feature I adore most about touchscreens. Once I find the appropriate seatmates, I sit down and open my book. Inevitably, after two or three stops, somebody sporting headphones or earbuds enters the train and plops down next to me. If the music is too loud, I nonchalantly close my book and wait a moment before getting up because I surely don't want to offend a stranger. Even more bizarre, I'm afraid they will know that I'm avoiding them if they see me strolling down the aisle in search of a new seat instead of leaving the train.

Fast and furious tapping on a laptop also takes its toll. A triple-seat change on a single ride is my average. My husband can immerse himself in the newspaper, unperturbed by his surroundings, and I'm sure he dreads riding public transportation with me. Honestly, it's not my fault that my circuitry is faulty.

Imagine if our cave dweller ancestors had blocked out all aural information with Paleolithic headphones. Predators would likely have hunted us to extinction. Humans possess binaural hearing, meaning we can pin down the whereabouts of sounds. This sure comes in handy when a car is skidding out of control or a Doberman is charging up the sidewalk. Bopping down the street to your favorite polka is not preferable to survival. Music should be uplifting, not lethal.

Electronic devices have altered human behavior. In today's world, privacy is passé, communication is constant, and emojis have replaced the intricacies of human feelings. And yes, I use them as well. I particularly like the pondering face. Anyway, once in a while, I crave some nineteenth-century sense and sensibility.

Aside from longing for the sound of silence, nutty conduct also gets my goat. One day, while enjoying a pleasant ride on a nearly empty train, a truculent woman on crutches entered the car. It was the beginning of summer, and the compartment was stifling. Nevertheless, she hobbled down the aisle on one crutch and slammed each window shut with the other, looking extremely pleased with herself. Then she plunked down on the seat opposite mine and said, "I don't like drafts."

Why couldn't I muster up some compassion for her phobia? Apparently, I'm only tolerant of my own shortcomings. Maybe we're all myopic regarding our own behavior.

It's time to grab your lap bars; the ranting coaster is approaching its final slope. First of all, when you find your leg jiggling like a sewing machine bobbin, try standing up. Sniffing like a truffle pig indicates the need for a tissue. Don't be shy, we're happy to help, but please, just blow. Do not honk. What's more, gum is not a percussion instrument. And I beg you not to pat your leg to the clearly audible beat. You're welcome to take an afternoon siesta, but remember, snoring ruins relationships, even among strangers. And for heaven's sake, cuticles are not dinner. Babies suck on body parts, grown-ups don't.

I thought about abandoning the subway altogether but swore off deodorant instead.

Weight Loss Forever

Recently, an ad in our local newspaper raved about a metabolic tracking device for losing weight. You blow into the gadget, and it uses your breath to calculate the number of carbohydrates and fat your body requires, then a message pops up on your phone, explicitly telling you what to eat. That's right, your love handles will disappear faster than you can say mint chocolate chip on a sugar cone, without exercise or calorie counting. It's that simple.

The fact is, food is powerful, and dieting is not effortless. I need to prepare for the challenges in life, and I can't tackle the job of dieting with a breezy attitude and a hundred-dollar breathalyzer. No app in the world will make abstinence fun. More information does not make up for less food. Weight loss is a science, but can the immense pleasure we get from food be measured? We are blinded by love for the crispy, the creamy, and the buttery. Sugar gets us high, and I'm not sure whether science is up to tackling this emotional powerhouse with logic and data. My smartphone can tell me what to eat, but it can't eliminate the pastry shop around the corner.

Losing weight is not a mystery that needs unraveling. Eat less, move more. Packaged fare will probably have more calories than food plucked from a tree or pulled from the soil. Go to a farmer's market and buy a five-pound bag of apples. You won't have to worry about binging on them while watching your favorite series. Never have I said to myself, this is your third apple, just stop already. Although, on one occasion, eating an apple was a real treat. While strolling through the Bavarian countryside with our seven-year-old son, we became hopelessly lost. Our hungry child spotted an apple tree laden with fruit, and we plundered it. Those stolen apples were hugely gratifying, but even a ravenous person can consume only so much fruit. A jumbo bag of chips, on the other hand, no sweat.

An overabundance of food surrounds us, and sustenance is never really an issue, but enjoyment is. We have choices, and that is the dilemma. When I'm famished, I'll eat anything. If I'm just in the mood for food, I'll eat whatever makes me happy. So, why not remove the options and emulate Tom Hanks in the film *Cast Away*. Tom plays a chubby pilot stranded on a remote island. Wilson the volleyball assumes the role of companion. After his plane crashes, flabby Tom washes up on the beach, and an hour later, our lean, lanky hero is showing off in a loincloth. Right about now, we pause the movie, make some popcorn, drizzle it with plenty of butter, and return to the living room to admire sexy Tom's spearfishing skills. We marvel at his handmade harpoon and think to ourselves, how impressive. I wonder whether I could accomplish such a feat.

Yes, you can, with my *Cast Away* diet. First, you pay my diet company a wad of cash, then I ferry you to a remote island and abandon you. Before disembarking, I'll provide you with a survival knife and a toothbrush. Although, if you are not successful with the knife, you won't need the toothbrush. Every day, you must forage and hunt for food. By the time you construct a harpoon, catch a fish, and build a fire, unless you prefer sushi, you will have expended more calories than the fish provides. Dessert is not an issue because you will be too exhausted to forage for berries. There is no science to the *Cast Away* diet; food remains an emotional experience, and not finding any would make you sad.

In the aftermath of a diet, we are eager to return to our former lives and are relieved that the misery of self-denial has finally ended. The truth is, we need to make lifestyle changes that last forever. So, I have a few tricks to jump-start your new way of life. For example, every time you reach for the cookie jar, pop a piece of licorice into your mouth, not that licorice-flavored corn syrup sweet you get at the candy store, but the real stuff that is black, bitter and made from licorice root. The potent taste of anise and fennel will put your taste buds into mourning, and the aftertaste will wreak havoc on your tongue for hours. Of course, mints will also work in a pinch. Along with the disgusting taste on the tongue trick, I make myself pay for junk food. Whenever I crave high-octane sugar, I need to eat something nutritious first, like an apple or a celery stick. Sometimes, I'm not in the mood for the naughty snack after the healthy one, but when I am, I look at it this way; at least I got a dose of fiber with my butter pecan sundae.

As for driving to a noisy, smelly gym to work out, I know I won't, so I've never joined a health club. Instead, I prefer riding a stationary bike in front of the television. The news gets me burning rubber, and at this rate, I'll be ready for the *Tour de France* after the next election.

At the end of the day, self-control has to be the dressing on our salad. In the 1960s, there was something called the Marshmallow Experiment. A psychologist offered four-year-olds a single marshmallow to be eaten immediately or two squishy sugar bombs if they waited fifteen minutes. It should come as no surprise that the kids who delayed gratification grew up to be skinny multibillionaires.

Go ahead, serve yourself a big portion of willpower, and calibrate your scales. Forever begins today.

Crime in Bavaria

I live in Bavaria, home of leather shorts, beer gardens, and alpine yodelers. We have about four thousand residents in our town, and unlike other places where I've lived, I never feel uneasy walking around after dark. We're not free of crime, but the countryside's bucolic sins rarely steal the show on the evening news. The local paper, more or less, tattles on the naughty. Assuming these stories weren't front-page news in your part of the world, let's take a look at a few of our most memorable crimes and misdemeanors.

One New Year's Eve, an inebriated twenty-seven-year-old man pushed his bike to a petrol station and attempted to fill it with gasoline. Just for the record, Bavarians cycle year-round and are never deterred by rain, sleet, or snow. A passerby happened to notice the rosy-cheeked cyclist and reported him to the police. The officers arrived and questioned him; however, the man was confident that he had driven his car to the gas station. I can assure you that my Schwinn has never resembled a Range Rover under any circumstance. To spare the cyclist the indignity of further humiliating behavior, the police incarcerated him and his bicycle. Three cheers for the kindly constables; they could have revoked his driver's license for drunk cycling. What's more, the good-natured attendant waived the seventy-four-cent fuel bill.

Gas station dramas certainly dominated the news that week. German law prohibits shops from opening on Sundays and public holidays. Still, people can satisfy their needs at gas station mini-marts, provided the markets sell only travel-related items. That's the entrepreneurial spirit! Of course, everyone knows there's more than just stale sandwiches and bitter coffee inside those dens of commerce. Unfair, cry retailers forced to remain closed. They are justifiably frustrated about losing Sunday revenue and are not shy about airing their grievances. "Convenience stores are raking it in, and we are being thrown under the bus."

True, but the fact is, only motorists purchasing gas are permitted to shop at the mini-mart. As was bound to happen, one Sunday afternoon, an errant gas station attendant sold a soft drink to a pedestrian. Outrageous as this sounds, undercover police were staking out that service station and witnessed the pedestrian leaving with the illicit soft drink. Instead of busting the guy, they swooped in and confronted the cashier. She did not deny her misconduct and even admitted to feeling out of sorts while selling the unlawful beverage.

"Today, we warn you. However, if you repeat this offense, a hefty fine awaits you," they told the repentant teenager.

Shopping is not the only activity banned on Sundays and public holidays. Noise pollution is also a no-go. Mowing your lawn may invoke the wrath of fellow residents and a hefty fine. One summer, after weeks of rain, our grass was knee high. Of course, the sun teased us on a Sunday, yet no one dared rev up the Toro. Humans are an odd bunch. A knee-high lawn would have been the crime where I grew up and not the sound of the mower. Occasionally, I risk raking leaves and sweeping the sidewalk during quiet time. Swishing is an innocent type of noise and not too unbearable, I hope. At least my neighbors have yet to chew me out.

Apartment dwellers must comply with even stricter noise taboos, including sexual fireworks. There's nothing worse than having your boisterous shenanigans annoy a testy neighbor. No wonder the population is declining.

One of my favorite childhood pastimes was fishing in Lake Erie. So, feeling nostalgic one Saturday morning, I said to Key, "Why don't we try catching our lunch at the nearby lake?"

"We can't fish without a license."

"Then we'll buy one at the bait shop. That's what my grandfather did."

"You can't just buy a license. You must take a course and pass a difficult exam. Another thing, fishing school is not cheap."

"You've got to be kidding."

"That's not all. Your license doesn't allow you to fish in every lake. You need to purchase a separate permit for each body of water."

"Sort of puts a lid on that kettle of fish."

A few weeks later, the newspaper ran a story about an immigrant caught red-handed with a carp. It just so happens that a member of the local fishing club was driving across the bridge and noticed a rod dangling over the railing. The man pulled over, got out of his car, and confronted the fisherman. The latter turned out to be a Polish immigrant without a fishing license. A single carp flopped in his styrofoam cooler. Unable to muster up some empathy, the sanctimonious meddler called the police. Wouldn't you feel tawdry reporting a poor man with a fish? Unfazed, the Pole holding the pole reeled in his second catch of the day. An officer arrived and questioned the immigrant, who unapologetically claimed hunger, not a love of fishing, motivated his behavior. Justice prevailed. The officer scolded the Pole, confiscated his rod, and tossed the man's dinner into the river. Regarding the fine, the felon was off the hook due to a crime in progress; hooligans were stealing clothing from the Red Cross donation bin.

After moving to Bavaria, I was shocked to discover that the German legal system is juryless. Instead, judicial power is entrusted to a panel of judges. In America, I grew up riveted to cameras panning across jurors' distraught faces during heart-rending testimonies. Television court was highly emotional, and I never questioned the unanimous vote of justice until now. Maybe there are disadvantages to having a jury, I reflected. Do I really want twelve individuals inconvenienced by my crime determining my fate? Chances are some of them will have the mental agility of a jellybean. Can we honestly expect people off the street to struggle with complex court proceedings and the subtle tactics of savvy lawyers? Judges, on the other hand, have sharpened their minds and debated countless litigations. You can argue that a judge is not objective, but at least he spent time cultivating fidelity to objectivity. What if a jury member is sitting in court contemplating their kid's soccer practice? I don't believe I could transcend my inadequacies, so it's a good thing I'll never be called to serve.

One afternoon, as I zoomed down a road ten miles per hour over the speed limit, the telltale flash of an automated camera recorded my infraction. A few weeks later, a blurry black-and-white picture arrived in the mail accompanied by an invoice for twenty-five euros. No matter how much time I have, there's always an urgency to my driving that I can't quite explain. But I'm not the only one in a rush around here. A pigeon was recently captured on film flying down a residential street at 45mph in a 30 zone.

What eye-rolling crime and punishment awaits us next week?

School

Considering how much time I've spent in school, I have substantial deficits. To begin with, my high school curriculum neglected things like insurance, contracts, taxes, and retirement accounts. Would teaching life skills alongside math, science, and history have been so inconceivable? For some reason, non-academic topics were taboo. The same goes for college. We learned nothing about music contracts, royalties, or performing rights.

When I was a child, the paperwork my father tackled every weekend remained a mystery. Whenever I asked him about it, he'd always reply, "I'm paying bills." What bills? I never thought to ask.

Of course, sex education got a notch on the totem pole, but what about navigating the jargon of a lease? It's a good thing they taught us to fear pregnancy because we sure never learned whether it was covered by insurance. Maybe it's time for schools to address the nuts and bolts of life. I'm sure the Magna Carta wouldn't mind sharing a seat with the disambiguation of mortgages.

The year I purchased my first health insurance policy, I had trouble imagining a scenario that would make my life collapse physically or financially. All I wanted was a cheap policy, and the agent obliged. My new coverage came with a huge deductible and no prescription coverage. The policy was as deficient as a loaf of white bread and should have come with a first aid kit.

Frankly, I saw no point in paying for a better policy until the day I twisted my ankle. I was playing tennis in running shoes, which, by the way, are designed solely for forward motion. While jumping sideways, my shoes applied the brakes and caused my ankle to rotate. I sure wish I had known about cross-trainers back then.

Accidents happen quicker than you can say out-of-pocket while the consequences linger. My ankle was swollen, bruised, and painful, yet an emergency room visit was not an option. The X-ray, exam, and compression bandage would have cost an arm and a leg. My lack of financial resources forced me to self-medicate with an ice pack and Tylenol. What did I learn from the incident? First of all, proper athletic footwear is indispensable. Second, pretending that a skimpy health insurance policy is adequate is like believing that corn dogs are nourishing.

Let's face it, reading a contract is about as appealing as skydiving without a parachute. I detest the vocabulary and idiosyncrasies of legally binding documents. Traversing the landscape of provisos, clauses, and stipulations, whether in a rental agreement or car insurance, is not intuitive. In school, we learned to write clearly and express ourselves concisely. Writing an intentionally confusing essay would have garnered a poor grade. And using twenty words when five would have sufficed usually made the teacher's red pen bleed. Likewise, she would have deemed it pretentious had we peppered our work with some bona fide Latin.

Years ago, because of ignorance, I signed away the rights to my work worldwide and forever. As I opened the envelope containing the contract from my first music publisher, my optimism was as bubbly as the bottle of prosecco beside me. I began reading carefully and methodically at first, but the legal gibberish put me into a coma, and before I knew it, I was merely skimming the agreement. I should have consulted a lawyer, but I'm afraid of them; they earn more per hour than I do in a week. Finally, confused and tired, I signed on the dotted line, officially relinquishing control of something I had created. You can't renege on an agreement once you've signed it, even when you realize it's unethical. Lawyers draw up contracts, and non-lawyers are expected to understand them. Can we put a moratorium on that?

Credit card debt is skyrocketing. Imagine if topics like interest rates, minimum payments, and balance payoffs were included in our schooling. We might approach that unwieldy piece of plastic with a little more fear and respect. Naiveté can ruin a life. Credit card companies invite, no, they actually coax us to spend more than we earn. We are seduced by rewards, zero interest, no annual fees, and a mouthwatering cashback policy. The good news is that your Kohl's dollars are tax free because cashback is considered a discount, not income. The variety of opportunities for saving by spending is stunning. We are remarkably gullible, which is why credit card companies love us.

The responsibilities of adulthood are overwhelming. A little preparation and awareness would go a long way. A shocking number of people live paycheck to paycheck and do not have retirement savings. Retirement is not an old-age issue, and you can't start thinking about it once you're wearing dentures. You should stash away ten percent of your earnings, starting with your babysitting money, unless you'd prefer waiting tables while shuffling behind a walker.

If I had a say in the matter, kids would burst into their life course classroom full of enthusiasm. The class would be moderated by a person who asked questions and guided discussions—kind of like Socrates. We'd kick off the semester with savory topics like a day at the stock market, etiquette anyone, and the unwelcome though necessary expense of health insurance. Then, students would explore, analyze, research, and debate everything from credit cards to social media behavior.

Of course, another option would be to integrate real-life issues into preexisting classes, like one of those math word problems we are so fond of. For example, Johnny opened his car door in the Costco parking lot, and a big gust of wind slammed it into the door of the neighboring Cadillac. The dent was three inches long and a sixteenth of an inch deep. Johnny's father recently adjusted his coverage and dropped comprehensive and collision. The ding in the Cadillac will cost more to repair than Daddy's yearly premium, which will rise significantly if he claims his son's mishap. Where will Johnny be working this summer?

Marten

Night after night, an intolerable weasel-like animal, also known as a marten, waits until we are sleeping soundly before bounding onto our roof. The thud of his landing invariably wakes us, and we lie in bed waiting for his ensuing routine. It's a real showstopper. First, Marty pries off a clay roof tile and squeezes into our house. Once inside, he scampers around the dead space above our bedroom ceiling before darting into the no man's land, entirely inaccessible to us. The previous owner built two small rooms in the attic and neglected to provide a human entryway to the crawl space, effectively creating a room for mice and martens.

Occasionally, the marten brings live prey into the house and forces us to endure the sound of defenseless birds being slaughtered and mice shrieking in the throes of death. We have a steeply pitched roof, and his antics occur mere inches above our pillows, so we kick the ceiling while lying in bed. At any rate, our stomping achieves nothing but a racing pulse, cold feet, and a sneering marten.

Suppose you are out for a stroll at three in the morning and pass our house. You'll hear us bellowing all sorts of expletives at this slender, agile, bushy-tailed mustelid, who is supposed to live in the forest with his mustelid relatives, the minks, badgers, and weasels. Apparently, martens don't enjoy residing in the woodlands and have moved to German suburbia to torment sleeping residents. Furthermore, they have a bizarre penchant for gnawing on automobile coolant hoses and spark plug wires. If your vehicle is a victim of a marten's escapades, you'll be saddled with a three hundred euro repair bill and most likely require a tow truck. I should mention that insurance will not cover this. Scientists and carmakers alike are baffled by the marten's culinary inclinations.

One night, I was in the bathroom when that intrepid animal began bustling around the window dormer. I grabbed a can of tub and tile cleaner, jerked the window open, and sprayed like a wild woman, "How's that for aromatherapy, you son of a badger!" The wind blew a mist of Shiny into my face. My burning eyes followed his fuzzy shadow, and to my surprise, he leaped onto our flat roofed garage and sprinted down the drainpipe.

"Now, I know your route," I hissed, shaking my Shiny.

A couple of years ago, we had a pair of doves nesting on the eaves above our bedroom window. They began cooing before dawn, and their droppings sullied our balcony. "I've had enough. We need a predator to scare them away," my husband announced. Then he stormed off to his workshop, plugged in the jigsaw, and crafted a life-size eagle from a scrap of wood. He painted the raptor black and hung it from the gable beam above our balcony. Every day, the bewildered doves sat on the ridge of our neighbor's roof and observed the twirling intruder. A week later, they disappeared, never to be seen again.

I know we sound heartless, so I must take a moment to explain. We own an untamed plot, and our lawn violates all rules of lawn ownership; mowing occurs monthly, not weekly. In fact, it's more of a meadow than a lawn. Dandelions and wildflowers completely eclipse the grass. Snakes and toads mingle among the goldfish in our pond, and insects are ubiquitous. Nature may roam freely in our yard, and anything that flies may inhabit the trees. However, the roof belongs to us.

"We got the doves to move on," my spouse said during breakfast one morning, "today, it's Marty's turn to find a new home. I'm carpeting the garage roof with chicken wire. Let him try to cross that road."

"Our victory deserves a toast. The prosecco is going in the fridge."

Key installed the chicken wire, and we celebrated a new beginning. That night, our furry gymnast must have vaulted over the hindrance because he landed on the roof with a louder than usual thud.

"We donate to the World Wildlife Fund. Our local bird conservation group accepts our help. It's Marty's habitat that we are saving, and this is how he thanks us."

"I'm wrapping barbed wire around the drainpipe," he answered gloomily.

"Remember the time Max tried to untangle a coil of barbed wire, and it sprang into his face and pierced his eyelid. Do you feel like visiting the emergency room with a roll of wire dangling from your face?"

"I'll be fine."

We purchased the wire, and my husband cloaked the drainpipe.

Marty was not deterred. That tenacious little freak found a new route and was darting across the roof the next night.

"Look at it this way, we might discourage burglars. The place is beginning to look rather seedy. Besides, he is probably jumping onto the roof from a tree branch. Marty is obviously not always climbing up the drainpipe."

"I've trimmed every branch within reach of the house. It was the first thing I did," he replied sullenly.

The next morning, we scoured the internet for solutions and discovered a thermal imaging wildlife camera. My spouse was intrigued and immediately ordered one.

"How is this supposed to help us?" I asked.

"I want to see how he does it."

Let him have his fun, I thought.

A few days later, the package arrived. You know, the novelty of the camera was a pleasant diversion. We installed it and waited—no marten.

"He hasn't bothered us for days. Obviously, the camera frightens him," I said excitedly.

"Let's not open another prosecco just yet."

Naturally, Marty returned around midnight. Our camera produced grainy footage of him pacing back and forth in front of the chicken wire before bounding across it on his stubby little legs. It was strangely satisfying to see him in action, and for a moment, we were almost proud of his acrobatic prowess.

Now what? An extermination website recommended weasel repellant powder. Supposedly, a whiff of the stuff is a real turnoff. I assumed if a bad-smelling person could make me change my seat on the subway, then perhaps this simple olfactory weapon was the solution. Clearly, they were preying on our desperation, but I ordered the useless dust anyway.

After that futile attempt, we purchased a solar-powered, motion-activated, electromagnetic rodent repeller. It made impressive clicking sounds; therefore, we knew it was working. Every night for a week, we changed its location and adjusted the buttons and dials. I might as well have swatted the marten with a rolled-up newspaper. The gadget was a flop.

For a brief period, we gave up. Then, a friend recommended using a live trap. The prospect of catching and driving Marty to the boonies was enticing. The day the humane trap arrived, we baited it with an egg and positioned it on the roof of the garage. Admittedly, we fantasized about sauntering over to the cage, smiling smugly and saying, "Well, look who we've got here. Your reign of terror is over!"

It turned out that the marten didn't like the egg, so we replaced it with baked chicken. Every morning, we peered expectantly into the trap. No marten.

"Either he's too afraid or too smart to go in," I told Key.

"Let's give it a few more days."

"Why? He's been ignoring the meat for nearly a week."

Marty eventually returned, and he never entered the trap.

Where there's a will, there's a way. I don't know who said that, but they were wrong. We surrender. Welcome home, Marty.

Sooner or later, it had to happen; Marty became a parent. After the kits arrived, yes, baby martens are called kits, the nocturnal rumpus escalated. Ironically, these bushy-tailed mammals are strangely romantic. They prefer copulating on moonlit nights and, apparently, can sustain relations for an hour or more. No matter how impressive this feat seems to be, the Nobel goes to a Swiss marten for shutting down the world's most powerful particle accelerator. The poor fellow chewed on CERN's electrical transformer, which caused a short circuit that led to a power outage at the Large Hadron Collider. It did not end well for him, and he received the award posthumously.

One day, I noticed water stains on the wallpaper in the attic and assumed the roof was leaking. I contacted a roofer who confirmed the leak and recommended replacing our six-ty-five-year-old clay tiles. "Now, the expense can be justified. Not only will the new roof be impenetrable for the marten, it will also be insulated, and I won't have to wear a jacket indoors all winter," I crowed.

Months later, the roofing crew arrived. After removing our tiles, they claimed they had never seen anything similar to our crawl space. It was littered with bones and feathers, and the 1950-era insulation was utterly shredded.

We've had our new roof for about a year, and I can tell you it is an unyielding fortress. Twice, our feisty friend attempted to crawl inside. Unsuccessfully.

Just a minute, I can hear my husband in the kitchen. I believe the Champagne cork is popping. Cheers, Marty.

Retail

Shopping was one of my mother's favorite pastimes. The glistening world of retail ignited her passion, and she relished the physical interaction with people and products. When she spotted a bargain, she was as ecstatic as a puppy, and garage sales got her pulse racing faster than a double latte. Paying a buck for something worth a whole lot more validated the effort of the hunt.

Very little about my shopping involves need. Necessity doesn't drive me to buy a new sweater, and I won't die of exposure because I must share the family jacket. Shopping is modern man's hunting and gathering, so if you think about it, searching for trendy jeans is in our genes. A snazzy appearance helps us survive in a stylishly competitive world. We can't show up to a job interview smelling like a mothball. A new suit renders confidence, while old stuff has a sell-by date and has lost its magic.

I prefer to shop for clothes in person rather than online because I am notoriously discerning about fabrics and fit. Comfort dictates every purchase. Itchy sweaters, as well as anything made from wool, drive me raving mad. I'm not too fond of tight clothes and would spend every waking hour in a muumuu if I were more daring. Moreover, I fail to comprehend why a T-shirt that will be washed out before it wears out must have scratchy plastic strips sewn into its seams. Not only do seam reinforcements tamper with my sanity, but nylon thread makes me want to wear my favorite skirt inside out.

Recently, a cuddly fleece jacket caught my eye, and I decided to try it on. No sooner had I inserted my arm into the sleeve than it began to itch. The manufacturers had lined the garment with coarse polyester. What is the point of putting the soft fabric on the outside? I don't want people to pet me; I want to be hugged by a viscose cotton blend. Truthfully, I can think of little else when clothing is annoying me. My intolerance also applies to perfume and turtlenecks. Why don't I join a nudist colony, you wonder? Because I am always cold.

No doubt about it, I enjoy romping around the online retail playground for non-clothing products. A while back, I purchased ten boxes of shiny black landscaping rocks from an online shop. My apologies to the delivery person. I would have bought stones from our local garden center, but they only stocked roughly hewn beige rocks and gloomy grayish chips. Rock My World touted stones in various colors, shapes, sizes, and textures. And let's face it, delivery to your doorstep is an unrivaled convenience, especially when the product weighs hundreds of pounds.

Appliances are also suited to buying sight unseen. One afternoon, I plugged in my iron and grabbed a cup of coffee while waiting for it to heat up. The phone rang, and I got so caught up in the conversation that I forgot about the sizzling fire hazard in the basement.

"That's it," I said to my husband, "I'm buying an iron with an automatic shut-off feature."

The next day, while browsing around our local electronics store, a young salesperson offered her assistance.

"I'm looking for an iron that shuts off automatically."

"Oh, they all do that."

"Nope, sweetie pie, they don't." I picked up a box. "Look, only this one shuts off after ten inert minutes; your other irons don't have this feature. Bogus information could result in someone's house going up in flames."

"Whatever," she replied, unfazed.

Hi-ho internet. I went home and found a dozen automatic shut-off irons in a rainbow of colors, and each appliance boasted a detailed product description. Countless strangers comforted me with their positive reviews. I have no idea why people take the time to write meticulous blow-by-blow reports of their experience with a product, but I bought my new iron based on a particularly favorable assessment. A quilter whose former iron scorched brown spots into the fabric wrote, "This iron is not too heavy, easy to clean, removes wrinkles in one sweep, and the automatic shut-off comes with a warning beep, which is invaluable since I alternate between pressing and sewing." Click. Two days later, it was on my doorstep.

Incidentally, our grandparents also enjoyed home shopping, except the Sears Roebuck Catalog was their mail-order playground. Of all things, they sold heroin in that innocent looking book of bargains. Just imagine, at the turn of the twentieth century, you could order a vial of opium as effortlessly as an ear trumpet. Try to match that, Mr. Colossus of retail.

Now and then, my mother would send one of her kids to buy cigarettes. People weren't uptight about selling tobacco products to minors in the seventies. My youngest brother started making cigarette runs at the age of ten. There he is, Kevin on his purple banana bike, zooming down the street full speed ahead to our rundown mom and pop store. He had a dollar in his pocket and a crumpled note saying, "Please sell my son a pack of Salems." The proprietor sold him the cigarettes without batting an eye.

Still, the hub of consumerism was up the road at the mall; an emporium brimming with shops, restaurants, a three-screen multiplex cinema, and an arcade crowded with teenagers. Quarters bulged from the kids' pockets, and they spent hours feeding hungry pinball and Pac-Man machines. Meanwhile, the power-strolling elderly scampered from one end of the mall to the other. Malls were suburban vacation islands. You could eat, play, and spend in a wonderland of perfect weather. Plus, your credit card company was more than willing to foot the bill. Just ask Giovanni Boccaccio, a fourteenth-century Italian writer, who perfectly understood the concept of credit when he said, "It's better to repent what you enjoyed than to repent not having enjoyed anything."

Since we're going back in time, let's take a look at an astonishingly modern multi-level shopping center showcasing a vaulted ceiling, exquisite marble floors, and an array of boutiques. No, I'm not talking about Vegas. I'm referring to Trajan's Market, built in Rome two thousand years ago. You might want to check out their food court. I just noticed a vendor dressed in a toga offering free samples of wild boar sausage.

We are drawn to shopping and the instant gratification it provides. Let us take a moment to thank our dopamine, that cunning neurotransmitter that keeps us begging for more. I don't know what the next shopping trend will be. All I know is that I'll be there by car or by mouse.

Salted, Sugared, Fried

Oblong sponge cakes infused with synthetic cream filling and marshmallows suspended in cake pans of green gelatin belonged to the culinary experiences of my childhood. On Saturday nights, I yearned for my parents to go out so I could enjoy a cryogenically frozen meal packaged in a compartmentalized aluminum tray. I marveled at the rectangles of reconstituted mashed potatoes, cubed carrots, and surprisingly crispy chicken, considering it was reheated in the oven and not pulled directly from a vat of grease. While sitting on the couch, watching a sitcom, I devoured my mouth-watering TV dinner at a foldable table. A sugary soda rounded off the meal. We rarely drank the unsavory Lake Erie water flowing from our tap. It had a nasty smell, especially during the summer, when it tasted like lukewarm aquarium water. Bottled water was not in vogue, and I'm pretty sure we grew up in a semi-dehydrated state. I don't know whether the repugnant taste stemmed from scores of dead fish, the annual toxic algae bloom, or the rampant industrial pollution pouring into the lake, but chlorine made it potable, if not palatable. Unfortunately, nothing could hide its off-putting smell, just like perfume can't really conceal the unwashed armpits of a down-to-earth bohemian shunning deodorant.

What can I say, TV dinners were intoxicating, and their grim lack of nutrition was inconsequential. During the 1960s, frozen and processed food usurped home-cooked meals. My mother adored their convenience and snazzy packaging. Our Thanksgiving pumpkin pie was concocted from canned brown mash, and pumpkins in their natural form existed solely for the pleasure of carving on Halloween. I was only vaguely aware that the pie I enjoyed with a dollop of imitation whipped topping was made from a vegetable. We omitted foods from our diet because we didn't like them, not because they contained gluten or lactose.

Like a stealth bomber, sugar's cheaper cousin, high-fructose corn syrup, ambushed our sustenance. We lapped it up in sodas, candy, and juice made with real fruit flavor. Foods that we assumed were healthy were loaded with sugar. Sound the trumpet for yogurt, that wholesome gelatinous glob atop a jellied lump of fruit. I'd like to talk about bread, but I'm getting choked up just thinking about it, so I'll share my ode to dough with you instead:

Oh, bread of wonders, you chemically fortified loaf
Who cares whether you have the nutritional value of a cotton ball
You are loved just the same
Go forth and fill yourself with peanut butter and jelly

Adieu, adieu, fluffy thing, because let me tell you, even as a child, I never liked you nor the jelly you concealed. The thought of eating peanut butter hidden by a congealed purple mass made me woozy. And therefore, I did not eat it, ever. I squished it inside my brown lunch bag and threw it away. At some point during grade school, I told my mother how much I abhorred that sandwich and pleaded with her to replace it with tuna on rye. She agreed. Finally, I didn't have to subsist on Crunchy Chunky until dinner. By the way, my favorite cereal was created by a flavorist who believed her breakfast concoction had a want-more-ishness quality to it. Doesn't all sugar have that attribute? I ate it nearly every day for eight years, and the pseudo ingredients mixed with artificial coloring and synthetic nutrients fueled my education in a kind of sick-ish way.

Welcome to the 1980s, the era of low-fat products. Supermarket packaging was decorated with colorful banners proclaiming heart-healthy, fat-free ingredients but forgot to mention their main ingredient, sugar. We traded high cholesterol for diabetes. 'They' coaxed us into believing that processed cookies, cereals, and cakes were good for us. My high school cafeteria served canned fruit cocktail, a popular dessert of plastic-looking fruit floating in syrup. When I was a child, we rarely ate unadulterated fruit. A spoonful of sugar brought out the best in strawberries, and apples were enhanced with a wrapping of caramel. A decade later, fruit was processed and pressed into colorful rolls. Sugar and artificial ingredients made it less boring than the produce grown on trees. Food was for tastin' good and fillin' up. We scoffed at vegetables. They were overcooked and enjoyed primarily by the toothless among us: babies and the elderly. Quite honestly, we would have rejected greens had they been lightly sautéed in organic olive oil.

We assumed an aerosolized imitation cheese product that sprayed goo through a nozzle perched atop its can was nutritious. Who needs healthy when you can have swirly decorations and fancy hors d'oeuvres in a spritz. Another brainchild of food engineers was a contrived cheese product that resembled a plastic brick but didn't look nearly as pretty on a cracker. I'm not saying I want to grind my own cornmeal, but maybe we could put the kibosh on pretend food.

These days, we can breastfeed our infants while browsing around a farmer's market. Well, at least we can sit in the car and do it. Grass-fed beef and free-range chickens not only have a higher quality of life than their cruelly raised, industrialized counterparts, but they also taste better. Superfood quinoa is not my cup of seeds. Nevertheless, its ubiquitous presence signifies progress. Poke bowls are replacing fish sticks and fries in the fast food lane. Investments in sustainable agriculture, ethnic cuisine, and organic supermarkets are booming thanks to venture capitalists. Cooking shows and blogs have opened our eyes to a new culinary experience. Thumbs up for quality and diversity.

Go ahead, check out potato recipes online, and discover just how versatile that humble root vegetable really is. And while you're at it, grab a cold craft beer and feast on a delicious episode of *Unforgettable Tubers*.

Trees

Paintings depicting majestic trees and rugged wilderness grace the walls of living rooms in my hometown. Yet, the majority of homeowners steer clear of similar displays in their own yards. With each passing year, visits to my parents' house became progressively unsettling because, for some inexplicable reason, the residents began eschewing trees. One year, the family across the street turned a hundred-year-old sycamore into wood chips, leaving behind a stump the circumference of a child's wading pool. I grew up with that tree, and the loss left me nauseous. The warblers that once lived in the sycamore flocked to our next-door neighbor's maple. Feathered tantrums and noisy battles ensued. Simply put, they were angry birds. You needn't be an ornithologist to recognize that the birds roosting in the few remaining branches around town were unhinged. Up the road, a little ornamental thing replaced a giant oak. Year after year, trees disappeared faster than you could say deforestation, and the last of the Mohicans became hopelessly overpopulated.

Over time, a ridiculous number of superstores framed by vast parking lots replaced the woods surrounding our Cleveland suburb. Myriad fast-food joints popped up like dandelions. Abracadabra! With a wave of his magic wand, the zoning commissioner transformed the suburban landscape into rolling plains of concrete and empty calories. But hey, we were rewarded with a nugget on every plate and a cheap pair of socks in every drawer. Trees vanished from our city, and deer, not the plastic decorative kind, moved to suburbia to graze on a plethora of geraniums. Isn't it odd to think that evergreens survived the meteor that wiped out the dinosaurs, and yet, a chain saw-toting lumberjack brings down a poem as lovely as a tree in about an hour.

One year, I fantasized about asking my parents' neighbors whether they would consider enhancing their vacant monoculture lots with trees, knowing full well that leaf raking would top the list of excuses. Then it occurred to me I wouldn't really be asking; in essence, I would sow a subconscious seed. Oh, I'm such a smarty-pants. The first neighbor I approached already had a small tree in her front yard. We stood side by side, admiring the sapling.

"Aren't wooded lots beautiful? They provide shade, and I bet they really reduce air conditioning costs," I said nonchalantly.

"Trees are pretty, but they sure make a mess in the fall."

"Look at it this way, raking provides excellent aerobic exercise. Just think what a gym membership would cost. Not only that, trees inhale gas fumes and produce oxygen, so we can breathe and not wheeze." Several leaves rustled in agreement. "As a matter of fact, I genuinely enjoy raking leaves," I prodded.

"It's been nice chatting with you, but I have to make lunch. Bye."

Having spent years searching for the perfect gift for my parents, I ditched the shaving cream warmer and began giving them trees—a magnolia for her, a mountain ash for him, and a dogwood for them. They never ended up at a garage sale, and like my mother's much-loved antiques, they improved with age.

Their house was camouflaged by a dense cloak of ivy. For decades, a single vine climbed the aluminum siding and sprawled its tentacles until it enveloped the entire edifice in a blanket of waxy green. The effect was stunning, and the facade was alive with mice, birds, and squirrels. Bees droned like a shruti box while imbibing the nectar of late-blooming flowers. My parents were inadvertently saving the bees before anyone realized they needed rescuing. Every autumn, copious berries attracted scores of birds to the all-you-can-eat ivy buffet.

In the land of barren lots, my parents were misfits. And yet, cars lingered at the stop sign in front of the house, admiring the yard. When my mother was outside, passersby often complimented her unconventional landscaping. You would think the neighbors would crawl out from underneath their mowers and follow suit. My parents' yard should have whet their appetites for more than just geraniums and ornamental lawn geese dressed in old-fashioned apparel. But people want surprises in their cereal boxes, not on their lawns, and uniformity prevailed. Too many fragile giants vanished from our city and our consciousness.

My grandmother lived in a tiny ranch house on the other side of town. Trees dominated her backyard, and uncultivated, shaggy ground cover crept around their trunks. I remember her birdbath being carpeted with algae. For some reason, untamed yards appear considerably larger than they are. My grandmother, an avid bird-watcher, was not evading maintenance; she simply preferred the company of trees to the monotony of grass. In fact, old lady status permitted her to veer from conformity without consequence. However, her front yard provided the prerequisite green rectangle, which my father dutifully mowed every other weekend. Each morning, I gaze out the window and savor a replica of her garden.

Have you ever wondered why you must squint to find trees in Greece, Malta, Scotland, and Iceland? I was amazed to discover the islands were swathed in voluptuous forests until ax-wielding humans arrived. Believe it or not, deforestation is nothing new. We have been changing the face of the planet for millennia. But, where, oh where, did all the logs go? Naturally, we had to clear forests to grow crops and for sheep to graze. The shipbuilding industry devoured innumerable trees to build vessels for travel, trade, and warfare. Pottery kilns and metal refineries were voracious log hogs as well. And think about it, humans have been cooking their food over wood fires for over a million years. Indeed, if you must chop down a giant oak to roast a mastodon, and you surely don't want to eat undercooked mastodon, why not gather a few acorns from the felled behemoth and plant them?

I'm guessing that short-sighted ignorance reigned far too long, and now it's payback time. Even Plato was fed up with his fellow ancient Greeks' deforestation excesses, and that was over two thousand years ago. The philosopher complained, "The Greeks wiped out the woods and left a mere skeleton of land."

Short of growing legs and fleeing, I don't know how trees can escape us. Of course, we don't have to hug them, but we could give them a pat on the bark once in a while and simply leave them be.

Say Cheese

Everywhere we go, we see people taking pictures, and they're not just commemorating the vacations and stations in life anymore. It turns out that ordinary events merit preservation for posterity as well. Fleeting moments are no longer transitory. Suppose I'm walking down the street and notice a snail creeping up a Porsche. I grab my phone and capture the irony. As I scroll through the hodgepodge of my digital albums and gaze fondly at a photogenic Caesar salad, I realize the camera is curating my memories. From Disneyland to a previously unrecorded storm cloud, life is lived through a lens and eagerly frozen in time.

The selfie stick may be new, but the concept is not. Artists have been depicting themselves for centuries. Rembrandt painted his likeness over ninety times. He even opted to smile for a few of his portraits, which was pretty radical in an era of widespread solemn expressions. As for the Mona Lisa,

I doubt that a mirthless Mona would have achieved such stardom. Her enigmatic smirk and missing eyebrows were her tickets to fame. I'm too antsy to pose for hours and would have been portrayed looking slightly annoyed, more of a Moaning Lisa.

Photographs of people I have never met but am supposedly related to wound up in a box in my parents' attic. The daguerreotype relatives of the nineteenth century are embedded on a metal plate. Nothing has been scrawled on the back, yet we claim them as our own. That picture rescued them from invisibility, but at the same time, it did not save them from eternal anonymity. Then there are the sepia-toned photographs, dated and captioned in elegant handwriting. We bear some resemblance to the ancestors depicted in those pictures, especially my grandmother as a little girl. Her face illuminates the family portrait, even though she and our forbears clung to the pensive gaze, the reigning look in pictures for decades. Actually, I would have been delighted to live in an era that didn't pressure you to smile for photographs. It's too bad straight-faced images didn't remain in vogue.

Had Instagram existed during the Victorian era, I bet you'd see a good number of post-mortem posts along with crying face emojis. Pictures of the deceased lying in coffins were all the rage in the eighteen hundreds. You'd also see aerial photos shot from the baskets of hot air balloons competing for likes with pictures taken by pigeons outfitted with itty-bitty cameras. Unbelievably, many of those birds got excellent footage before flapping home, unless they were shot down and eaten, as sometimes happened during the Second World War.

My father's source of pride was his 35mm Argus camera. When it was time to commemorate an event with a picture, my mother eagerly herded the family into the living room and lined us up in front of the fireplace. We dreaded the photographic process. It began with my father pulling a light meter from his pocket and communing with the room's illumination. Shutter speed was of the essence; time was not.

"Dad, we're gonna be wearing dentures by the time the camera is ready."

"I'm almost finished," he'd say, and continue to adjust various dials and lenses. Then, just when we thought it was time to look amused, he'd pull a flashbulb from his pocket, and we'd exchange looks of exasperation as he pushed it into the socket. "Say cheese," my mother chirped a moment before the flash erupted and rebounded off our retinas, leaving us in a cartoon sketch of floating blue dots.

Each photo was calculated and significant. The cost of buying and developing film kept photographers choosy and frugal. Crummy pictures cost the same as decent ones. Today, I have more photos on my hard drive than are hanging on the walls of the Louvre, which is thirty-five thousand, by the way.

One year, my mother picked up a Polaroid camera at a flea market. Polaroids are magic cubes that spit out grainy photos in minutes. Instant gratification aside, our infatuation with the camera was short-lived. Polaroid cameras are portable darkrooms and cumbersome to lug around. Therefore, we banished it to a limbo room such as the attic, basement, or closet, where it could fulfill the (you might need it) waiting period before being sold at a garage sale.

Not so long ago, all cameras were analog, and their film had to be developed into prints or slides. For about a decade, my father preferred the crisp resolution and superior quality of slides. Still, there was nothing spontaneous about viewing them. You had two options: hold the transparent two-inch square of film up to a hot light bulb or wait for slideshow night, which occasionally happened on Saturday nights and, despite recurring a thousand times, never lost its charm, a little like Christmas. We'd haul the screen and projector down from the attic and turn our living room into a theater. Year after year, we savored the same images. Without fail, it made us laugh to see my brother asleep in his high chair, holding a half-eaten hamburger.

Instamatic cameras made their debut in the sixties. They were small, inexpensive, and easy to use, yet they still relied on film. My father resisted the Instamatic. His kids did not. All of us received cameras as gifts for one occasion or another, and our prints accumulated in boxes and drawers. The Instamatic made us less discerning, resulting in quite a few chopped-off heads, faceless silhouettes, and grainy landscapes. You never knew what your roll of film harbored until you sat on the stoop of the drugstore, ripping open an envelope stuffed with expensive, crappy photos. At the moment, my old camera, replete with half-used film, sits abandoned in our attic graveyard next to a mechanical typewriter and an eight-by-ten sepia photograph of my husband's ancestors.

Hello, digital cameras. Three cheers for crop, edit and delete. Imagine, now, you could take thousands of pictures and erase the lousy shots. Nevertheless, digital breeds greed, so last year, I organized our plethora of pixels. Nothing had been erased in over a decade, and I could have churned butter for the entire town in the time I spent sorting through the clutter. My eyes ached, and my brain craved a massage, but I didn't stop until the task was complete. Then, my impetuous inner voice said, "While you're at it, why not digitize all your old negatives?"

Of course, I bought a scanner and spent countless hours shoving long gray strips through a slit in the machine, effectively giving birth to a new digital heap.

My camera icon is sandwiched between a flashlight and a weather app, and its absence is unimaginable. I take pictures on a whim, then erase or share them with a click. And this powerhouse of technology fits in my pocket. As far as I'm concerned, photography is right up there with a walk on the moon.

The Pond

The time had come to tear up our front lawn, chop down our arthritic pear tree, and replace it with a pond. Properties in Europe are small and pricey, so front and back yards are equally utilitarian, and since there are no neighborhood associations enforcing conformity, you can do whatever you like with your yard. Rivers of grass don't flow between houses; yards are enclosed by fences, walls, and hedges, and in our case, we have all three. I never sunbathe, but should my tolerance for toasting myself ever change, I could easily bask au naturel.

Ponds should be at least five feet deep if your fish are to survive the winter. And in the spirit of do-it-yourself homeowners, we were hell-bent on digging the hole ourselves. All I can say is never underestimate the consequences of overexertion. When you constantly mistreat your vertebrae, you better know a doctor who has a knack for cortisone injections.

After digging the hole and lining it with vinyl, we filled the pond with water. Then we added entirely too many goldfish and water lilies. With no one to reign us in, we went wild planting flowers, bushes, and ground cover along the perimeter. The whims of nature took over, and before long, the garden resembled a jungle.

Long-legged water striders and mosquito larvae joined the birds, butterflies, and bees in our idyllic habitat for a round of sex and metamorphosis. Following d'amour, insect hotels and birdhouses provided excellent accommodations for raising a family. Despite the abundance of life, we wanted more, and like addicts, we brought a constant parade of plants and animals into our suburban utopia. "I heard that bivalves make great filters," Key said. And then, he tossed a giant freshwater mussel into the pond. A certain satisfaction came from watching it sink.

Unbound by rules, dandelions and wildflowers mingled among the clover and overgrown grass in our backyard. A pile of leaves served as a hideaway for the resident hedgehog. Every night, our simple-minded dog poked his nose into its prickly quills, yet the pain never improved the spaniel's learning curve. That being said, we were not about to evict the hedgehog just because the dog was too foolish to leave it alone.

Let's visit the backyard villa my husband built for our two female dwarf rabbits. Bunny Land is on the ground floor, and if you climb the ladder, you'll find a playhouse with hardwood floors and a hornet's nest, which we'll remove in the fall after it's abandoned.

I've never excelled at math, but shall I tell you when one plus one equals ten? When pet shop owners cannot tell the difference between male and female rabbits. It turns out that Sarah and Francine were really Sarah and Freddy. In no time at all, our bunnies dutifully fulfilled the expectations connected with their species. Lacking the means to expand, we kept the parents and two kittens. At least, that is what taxonomists call them. In the end, the bungling pet shop agreed to take the rest of the litter, but only after we paid the vet to verify their good health.

The game-changer occurred the day my husband and son collected jellied clumps of frog eggs from a friend's pond and released them into our overcrowded body of water. The embryos filled me with foreboding. Perhaps not all will survive the transition, I mused. Frogspawn must be fragile, right? A few days later, the eggs hatched, and thousands of sperm-like tadpoles turned our pond into a giant womb.

I must admit, I sat on the swing and waited for hungry predators to partake in the buffet. Once, a crow landed on the marshy edge and scooped up a snack, but it made no noticeable difference. Day after day, the neighbor's cat crouched on a rock and swooped ineptly at the mouth-watering spectacle. If there were other customers, I never saw them.

Unleashing plants and animals into a foreign environment often causes dysfunction. Some years ago, a man living on a tropical island tossed an unwanted, exotic houseplant into the stream behind his house. The plant, which turned out to be invasive, floated downstream and triggered a devastating chain reaction. It took root, and as it grew, it blanketed the hillside and deprived the native tree saplings of sunlight. As a result, they died. Without mature trees, the slope lacked a stabilizing root system. In the wake of heavy rains, a mudslide sent a torrent of ochre soil into the ocean, annihilating untold marine life. Eventually, the rogue plant invaded the remainder of the island and wreaked havoc on the entire ecosystem. An innocent act culminated in irreparable calamity.

Our pond's fate wasn't as catastrophic. Even so, one night, the good fairy waved her magic wand and transformed the polliwogs into almond-sized froglets. We awoke to a scene that was biblical. The stone paths were alive, and every step had to be taken with caution. No matter how carefully we tread, we couldn't avoid flattening a few youngsters. I have no problem snuffing out a fly with one swat, though trampling a baby frog is another story.

When it rained, the lawn looked like it had fleas. Mowing was out of the question. It's one thing to step accidentally on a tiny frog and quite another to hack it up with a lawnmower blade. A few adventurous froglets hopped down the steps leading to the backyard, but their infant legs could not leap high enough to return to the pond. "I'm sure they'll find a way," I said to my husband.

Frogs are ancient creatures. Their ancestors hung out with the dinosaurs, and when a fatal asteroid struck our planet sixty-six million years ago, dinos were reduced to fossils, and frogs not only survived, they thrived. That is until we stepped into the picture. Today, frogs are croaking en masse from pesticide-laden waters, fungal diseases, and automobile traffic.

Frogs are the beloved stars of fairytales and predictors of rain. In China and Japan, they bring good luck. In France, they're an appetizer. In our yard, they were a challenge. Still, we remained attached to them.

One night, the entire menagerie disappeared, never to be seen again. To this day, we don't understand why.

In any case, it was time to sit Key and Raphael down for a family powwow. "No more uninvited guests," I quacked. "Do you hear me?"

Yeah, they heard me, but I know they weren't listening.

Brassiere Almighty

Anyone who wears a brassiere understands the quest for the perfect undergarment. Truth is, I'm an underwire bra abstainer and cannot understand the widespread fondness for shaping the bosom with rigid wire or molded plastic. Even the thought of wearing an undergarment that burrows into my rib cage makes me cringe. For the most part, I've given up fighting gravity's relentless downward pull. Look at men's briefs. They don't boast a supportive crescent-shaped strip of metal embedded in the fabric. Would a man expose his dangly parts to such an inhospitable environment? Boxer shorts are merely refined loincloths. It's no secret that men enjoy all things wireless.

I realize that quite a few women are undaunted by the strips of metal sewn into the supportive cups' fabric. Still, if you ever need a defibrillator, you better have someone remove your bra before jolting you back to life because wires can cause burns. Then again, bullets have ricocheted off wires in bras and deflected knives in stabbing attacks. If you travel to East Africa, do not wear an underwire bra because the tumbu fly might have a rendezvous with your shapewear. This insect has been known to deposit its eggs in clothing, and for some reason, it is quite fond of the underwire bra. If the fly mates with your brassiere, parasitic larvae will hatch from the eggs and invade your unbroken skin. The maggots will then feed on your tissue. This might ruin the quality of your vacation, but hey, you'd have an Instagram photo receiving unrivaled views.

Since the seventh grade, I've been searching for the perfect brassiere and am determined to find one before I die. I won't sacrifice comfort for beauty; therefore, I will never be issued a *Pretty Lady* rewards card. Instead, I prefer to lift myself up with a stretchy, seamless, cotton microfiber blend that glides like a second skin over my bust. My undergarments are not trimmed with scratchy lace, and I don't look like a pretty package worthy of unwrapping, but I am bolstered by the bliss of comfort. Unless the manufacturer sews itchy nylon thread into the under band, which I can tolerate for a few minutes before ripping the dreadful garment from my body while cursing its creator.

Padded bras are sculpted landscapes, intended to bestow the wearer with complete control over the bosom's shape, size, and bounciness. The possibilities are endless. We have the molded cup, the push-up, which would give a flat-chested man cleavage, the gel bra, and my favorite, the prominent bullet bra of the 1950s. Two pointy mountains rise from the torso's wilderness, and the cone-like projections stretch over a tight pastel sweater, eclipsing all other physical features. If you've had the good fortune to be endowed with mammaries capable of feeding triplets, your ornamental mountains scream, climb me.

Bras that embellish our physical attributes also enhance self-confidence. An undergarment that has the power to nourish the envy of women and the desire of men deserves respect. In Germany, the provocative *büstenhalter* boosts boobs and tips, especially for waitresses working at the Oktoberfest. When waitressing for this event, women of all ages pour themselves into the tight, revealing ethnic dress of the Alps called a *dirndl*. The form-fitted bodice and plunging neckline are typically worn with a low-cut, lacy white blouse that emphasizes the décolletage. Puffy sleeves enliven the girly effect, and an antler brooch placed strategically below bountiful titties drives men wild. The waitress descends upon a table of drinkers, carrying a tray laden with foamy mugs of Pilsener. Condensation pearls on the glasses and mouths water as the jiggly bosomed goddess approaches. She leans over the table, provides a teasing view, and distributes the refreshment. The job is grueling, but the push-up bra helps her earn in two weeks, what some make in a year. Let's face it, bras have superpowers.

It's difficult to imagine that women of the sixties burned such an omnipotent garment. I would like my bosom to stand for women's rights and not sag for them. Nowadays, female bra entrepreneurs are raking in millions in profits, and the global lingerie market brings in over thirty billion a year. Bullet bras are out, and sports bras are in. The possibilities are infinite, and the allure of bras has never been more tantalizing. So, the industry is boobing, I mean booming. Men's underwear is often displayed in the corner of the pajama department, whereas women's intimates receive an entire floor. Predictably, we need more time to shop.

Years ago, I found a comfortable, if not perfect, brassiere. Fortunately, I bought quite a few of them. Once white, they have acquired that bluish-gray color unique to old underwear. It's an irreversible color. Bleaching only adds a yellowish hue to the already lusterless garments and makes them smell like a public pool. Occasionally, I lumber around lingerie departments, dumbfounded by the prices, but I would pay anything for the perfect brassiere.

Out of curiosity, I once picked up a thong. The headband I use to wash my face is more substantial than this flimsy wisp of underwear. I might as well go tribal; it would certainly be cheaper. Maybe one day, I'll turn my old lace tablecloths into undergarments and sell them on Etsy. In the meantime, I will cling to the hope of finding the ultimate brassiere.

Courage

Americans have bonded over a large, waddling North American bird for over three hundred years. Our loyalty to that feathered creature and its must-have side dishes is astonishingly unbending. In the spirit of fellowship, we, the descendants of pilgrims, reap our Thanksgiving harvest at Whole Foods and take our culinary assignments seriously. So how on earth do a few shrewd guests avoid pitching in year after year without a trace of regret? Liberated from toiling in the kitchen, they idle away the morning sipping coffee and watching the Macy's Parade. Tom, the animatronic turkey, provides hilarious entertainment while the rest of us labor in front of hot stoves splattered with grease.

One year, a friend who had promised to bring a sweet potato casserole showed up on our doorstep after breakfast and unapologetically handed me a bag of dirty yams. Then she said, "Could you make the casserole? I really don't have time today. By the way, the sweet potatoes are organic." I smiled and said, "You've got to be kidding me." She ran off, and I launched a potato at her fleeing backside. Of course, that's not true at all. I said, "Yeah, sure," and stomped into the kitchen, yelling at the turkey. "Such an entitled princess. She can't foist her responsibilities on me."

"Well, she did, and it's too late now, gobble, gobble. By the way, I'm the victim here, not you."

That evening, when the mageirocophobe arrived, believe it or not, mageirocophobia is a fear of cooking, I took her coat and embraced her before offering her crispy-skinned turkey and fluffy mashed sweet potatoes. Then, after a few glasses of wine, I plucked up the courage to send her nasty telepathic messages.

I'm not sure why we brood in the back seat and permit, no, encourage others to navigate our lives. Barking is unnecessary. A simple no will do. Give and take, sure, just not take and take. Reciprocity must be a virtue because it sure doesn't seem to be a social norm.

I remember unfondly the summer my daughter's friend invited her on a week-long family camping vacation. Shortly before their departure, the parents called to request three hundred dollars for food, campsite, gas, and road tolls. Did I pay that outrageous sum? You bet I did. For two reasons: our kid had committed to the trip, and I'm about as courageous as a goldfish.

As it happens, the previous summer, we wined and dined their child in my mother-in-law's Tuscan country house and sent her home bearing gifts, specifically, extra virgin olive oil pressed from fruit we harvested from dawn until dusk the previous fall. It seems the parents should have been reminded of this small detail, and it looks like I was too gutless to mention it. We often sugarcoat responses that require toughness. Why? Because unexpected requests catch us off guard, and most of us will do anything to avoid an altercation. When a mosquito is sucking our blood, we promptly smash it, but we sure don't want to offend a human parasite.

Do you know what makes me howl? Not out loud, of course, I might hurt someone's feelings. People who wedge themselves in line at the grocery store pretending not to notice the patient customers waiting stoically behind them. I refuse to tolerate such impertinent behavior and hurl silent curses at the offender. "May your milk be curdled, you ill-mannered lout." Oddly, my internal rants do nothing to dilute my frustration. The path of least resistance is often paved with resentment.

Fortunately, desperation is emboldening. The summer I turned twenty-one, I worked as a clarinetist in an Italian opera orchestra. The musicians were compensated weekly and housed with local families. Our salary covered little more than meals. After the first rehearsal, I stopped at a deli to buy bread and cheese and paid with a large lira banknote equivalent to one hundred dollars. The guy at the register gave me change for a ten. At first glance, it looked like a lot of money, but it wasn't. He left me with a few bucks to live on for the rest of the week. "You didn't give me the correct change signor," I said. He shrugged. For the first time in my life, I had no choice but to fight. My ensuing tirade showered him in spittle, yet he still refused to correct the deficit. And to make matters worse, he stood there smirking. Crossing my arms in front of my chest, I said, "I will not stop squawking until you give me the proper change." The crook opened the register and dropped the money into my shaking hand. Years later, the Italian government required every proprietor to issue a receipt, even for a thimbleful of espresso. It appears that tourists weren't the only ones being swindled by shopkeepers.

Courage is the vehicle that drives our reactions, and it can't always be summoned at a moment's notice. Our inner hero emerges when it's a matter of life and death; conversely, courage tends to nap on the periphery when confronted with an innocuous circumstance. As was the case the day I was walking through our village with a friend. The sidewalk was narrow, and the bordering hedge encroached on the pavement, so we walked in the street. A street, I might add, that was about as bustling as the South Pole Highway. A passing car stopped and waved me over. "I bet he needs directions," I said to my friend. As I approached the vehicle, the driver began ranting, "Why are you walking in the street? You should use the sidewalk." Boy, was I mad. I grabbed the baguette I'd been clutching under my arm and thumped that belligerent motorist over the head. No, I didn't. I let it go. It was not worth ruining my baguette. I mean, remaining levelheaded is also a sign of courage, isn't it? Berating him would have resulted in a jousting match, and he would have ended up covered in breadcrumbs.

When all is said and done, "It's better to be a lion for a day than a sheep all your life," human being extraordinaire Elisabeth Kenney once said. She also had another insightful notion, "He who angers you conquers you."

Credit Cards

Not surprisingly, money inspires confidence, but procuring money instantly is pure magic. The birth of credit cards unleashed a tsunami of indulgence, and emancipation from the confines of cash changed our lives forever.

My grandparents were credit card skeptics. Borrowing money was right up there with sex; you did it only when absolutely necessary. As children of Polish and Lithuanian immigrants, they never bit off more potato kugel than they could chew. Above all, they owned property. Their meticulously maintained bungalow boasted a lawn that resembled synthetic carpeting, and their Buick looked untouched by time. Without fail, my grandfather polished the car weekly, and under no circumstance was food ever consumed in that vehicle. Understatement shaped their lives, and their modest income made them cautious. But most importantly, possessions were regarded as a privilege, not a right.

My mother embraced credit cards with tears of joy. Charge cards spun straw into gold and spawned her love of shopping. Omnipotent debit and credit cards were the ultimate enablers of commerce and made waiting for things passè. Buy now and worry about the bill later or not at all. Of course, paying bills was my father's job, and I'm sure he denounced that ruinous piece of plastic every time he wrote a check.

Nevertheless, the intoxicating cornucopia of retail was a downright feast, and everyone had a seat at the table. Spend your limit was the motto of the hour. Yes, indeed, the multitudes were determined to have some rainy-day fun at the mall before they were too old and senile to get high on shopping. "Who needs a nest egg when you have me," cried the card.

In the early days, using a charge card was not an unbridled adventure. Your credit balance had to be verified by a merchant before your new silk nightie could leave the store. Authentication was a time-consuming endeavor. Eventually, Visa computerized the process, and transaction time decreased to less than a minute. Vive le shopping. You only live once, baby, and if you die in debt, the credit card company can howl at the moon for their money.

Shopping is a tonic for what ails us and a diversion for what bores us. When you get right down to it, a sense of achievement often accompanies a beloved purchase. To say nothing of the scads of malls and online shops fostering our browsing and spending appetites.

Markdowns persuade us that a penny saved is a penny earned. You may spend fifty bucks to save a dollar, but at the same time, you generate points and will soon be able to stay at a hotel for free. Yes, free! Never mind that you racked up ten thousand dollars in credit card debt for a night in an eighty-dollar room. Everything you bought was essential and on sale.

One dreary Sunday afternoon, you kill time browsing around your favorite furniture store. You don't need new living room furniture, but you sure want it. The leather recliner you've been eyeing for a year is begging to come home with you. Let's be honest, the tufted sofa and nesting coffee tables would look fabulous next to that chair. The salesman has been watching you, and like a jaguar hunting a rabbit, he knows when to pounce. Big kitty struts over to the recliner and strokes it. His buttery sales voice coos, "If you buy this living room set today, you don't need to make a payment for twelve months. Zero interest." This man has just freed you from the shackles of saving up for merchandise. Don't pet the kitty, honey.

"That's an amazing deal, but it's still expensive, and I don't really need it."

"Tell you what, buy now, and I'll take off ten percent."

You hesitate because your mislaid commonsense kicks in.

"Let me think about this for a minute. I buy a sofa, recliner, and coffee table today. Then, I sit, eat, and spill drinks on this furniture for a year. The dog sheds on it. Occasionally, Mr. Fido wets it. After it looks ready for the thrift store, the first payment is due. But I don't want to pay for old, used furniture, and besides, what if my fridge breaks down and the hot water tank quits? I'll be left high and dry."

The jaguar has been kicked by the bunny and slinks away.

Credit cards make us reckless. It's easy to make foolhardy purchases with someone else's money. I usually pay cash for necessities, like socks and deodorant, but the fun stuff goes on the credit card. That way, I can live guilt-free until the bill arrives.

Do you know who I envy? The nomadic families you see on National Geographic living in yak-wool tents. (Not to be confused with circular yurt dwellings). Furniture may be on their wish list, but they don't have time to shop. Spinning all that yarn into a mid-sized abode takes about a year, and after that, they must get down to the business of weaving goat hair rugs to sleep on. Being dirt poor doesn't necessarily mean you enjoy sleeping on dirt. Granted, the kids of the Tibetan plateau wouldn't mind playing soccer in two-hundred-dollar shoes, except they are busy churning butter, making soap, and rubbing their dusty garments on a washboard. I hope these activities instill euphoria because romping around the mall is not an option. How on earth do they survive without oodles of fun products?

Credit card companies compel you to sin and then demand atonement. How messed up is that? Last week, a friend of mine received the following letter:

Dear Valued Customer,

We understand your craving for chicken vindaloo at an overpriced restaurant. Nevertheless, that meal was the papadam that broke the camel's back. So, we're writing to remind you, for the umpteenth time, to pay a little something toward your balance. Your late fees are piling up, and let me put it this way, with the interest you've accrued, you could have flown to India for that meal. Remember, you signed a lengthy and bewildering contract when you applied for this card. Of course, you didn't understand the agreement, but you definitely got the gist of it. We gave you a two-thousand-dollar spending limit, and we expect it back. And honestly, eighteen percent interest is fair compensation for our kindhearted generosity. If you cough up two percent of what you owe, you'll be debt-free in just three hundred and forty months or thirty years.

Sincerely,

Bob

A middle-aged guy who hates his lousy job.

Flat Earthers

The other day, I was bowled over by an article claiming that some of my fellow *Homo sapiens* believe the Earth is flat. On second thought, flat-earthers don't like to be called that, so let's refer to them as Neanderthals instead. Never mind that Aristotle proved we eat, pray, and love on a big, round ball. But, heck, what do dead people know? For whatever reason, flat-earthers have contorted our globe into a planetary pie plate and plunked the North Pole smack dab in the middle. Today, at the supermarket, I picked up one of those novel flat peaches and thought; I bet the spherically challenged prefer them. You know the old adage, flat peaches for a flat world.

Here's a question for you, flat-earthlings, "Why don't our oceans spill over the planet's edge?"

"Everyone knows that water does not cascade over the brim like an enormous waterfall because Antarctica, the frozen wall of ice that surrounds the circumference of our humble slab, holds it in."

Platygaeans may be divorced from logic, but their arsenal of answers is certainly colorful.

"Then why, may I ask, hasn't commerce exploited the ice belt? Cruises to the edge should be thriving. Surely, edge-of-the-earth paraphernalia would be all the rage. We'd have glass elevators racing up the ice wall to disk-top gift shops. And Vimeo users would be wowed by videos shot from the helmets of hang gliders dropping into the abyss of space? Can you explain why Facebook and Instagram aren't suffocating us with edge-of-the-earth selfies? You can purge your trembling brains of science, flat-earthlings, but if your vacuous fairytales were true, YouTube would be bursting with proof."

"Don't get me started. You globoids control everything, including social media. And for heaven's sake, just admit that you've erased our videos and photoshopped the planet into a sphere. By the way, it's common knowledge that the military is blocking the entrance to the edge."

As far as I can tell, the scientifically immune have been around for centuries. In 1543, Copernicus discovered that the sun was at the center of our solar system. He published his findings, but the church disapproved and banned his book. Nearly a hundred years later, the astronomer Galileo used his telescope to prove that Copernicus was right on the money. This time, the church brandished the Bible and proclaimed that the Earth was the center of our cosmos because God made the Earth the center of all things, and scripture proved it to boot. I'm not sure when or how God told this to earthlings, but Galileo politely reminded the church that the Bible was an authority on faith and morals, not science. That school of thought did not sit well with the church, and they placed Galileo under house arrest for his heretical beliefs. The punishment was pretty lenient since torture was at the top of the retribution list for blasphemy.

Flat-earthers scamper gingerly across our slice of terra firma spewing nonsense. Still, believing in Santa never hurt anyone. Who cares if a few people think the world popped out of a toaster. However, when climate change skeptics insist that carbon dioxide doesn't cause global warming, the consequences of this notion impact every creature on our sullied globe. We are making a mess of this place, and denying this is like saying that cheesecake is an asset to a weight loss program. In fact, you can validate anything online. For instance, try another weather app when you're unhappy with a forecast of rain. You are bound to find some sunshine.

Physics and math are complicated topics and often trigger fear. I panicked before every high school algebra class. Math made me miserable, and I still suffer from post-mathematic stress disorder. Basically, there are two kinds of people: those who slap a fake sticker on science and those who don't. As a physicist, my son collects data, analyzes it, and draws conclusions. In many ways, interpreting data and interpreting language are similar processes. Go ahead, choose a word, and open your thesaurus. Just for the heck of it, I looked up the word thesaurus in my thesaurus. Onomasticon is one synonym. Treasury of words, which is more poetic yet equally accurate, is another. Scientists are on a quest for knowledge and aren't claiming moral authority. They are merely trying to improve our lives.

Though it may seem like small potatoes, what you cook for dinner profoundly affects the environment. Even if you live on a flat planet. Yesterday, I decided to make shrimp fajitas. The grocery store stocked a cheap variety of shrimp and pricey organic ones. The low-cost crustaceans were raised in Thailand in appalling conditions. What's bad for the shrimp is bad for us, right?

"Party pooper," shrimp lovers on a budget cry. "Cheap doesn't always imply low quality." In this case, it does. Mucky shrimp farming ponds have replaced pristine mangrove forests. We don't need bargain shrimp, but we do need mangroves; they absorb carbon dioxide and act as nurseries for baby fish. Plus, and this is important, their aerial roots help prevent erosion and flooding, and the trunks reduce the impact of waves, especially during a tsunami.

Furthermore, shrimp peelers are often children and impoverished migrants forced to endure grueling sixteen-hour shifts and physical abuse. Our pan-seared citrus prawn dinner is served on a plate of human trafficking and decimated forests. If we can afford to eat shrimp, we probably have the means to shell out for organic.

Flat-earthlings may be cosmically challenged, but we're wired for denial and self-deception. Let's face it, sometimes reality is inconvenient. Although, I'm not sure what flat-earthers gain by being intellectually tethered to a terrestrial frisbee. Perhaps a ride on a lot of hot air.

The Exhibit

A few years ago, I attended a friend's installation at a prestigious art museum in Munich. Frankly, I was impressed that he was discovered during his lifetime. Van Gogh sold only one painting before committing suicide, yet his death was the launching pad for a long and lucrative career. As a matter of fact, his *Portrait of Doctor Gachet* was sold by Christie's for eighty-two million dollars. The bidding jumped in twenty-million dollar increments and took all of three minutes. Broke and undiscovered, the artist painted the picture a few weeks before his death. In my book, it is far more devastating to be denied appreciation than to be poor.

Installations have been around since the late nineteen-sixties. The aim is to alter a space creatively. A conceptual artist supplies a vision and doesn't hover over an etching or chisel away at a marble slab. Anything goes; you can fill a room with cellophane and old newspapers, and if a curator thinks it's grand, you have a gig. Christo, a famous conceptual artist, wrapped the German parliamentary building in silvery fabric and tied it with blue rope. The dressed-up parliament building was wildly popular and attracted around five million visitors, but it could have had a different outcome. Art is always a gamble, and the artist goes it alone. Uniformity is safe, art isn't, and installations are full of surprises.

The day of our friend's vernissage, I went into my bedroom and stared at the clothes in my closet. Should I go for an elusive chic, boring classic or a bold, artsy look? I opted for a long-sleeved asymmetrical black sweater and tapered black pants. But after seeing myself in the mirror, I jazzed up the outfit with a white leather belt, which made me look like an Oreo cookie. The line between artsy and clownish is as blurry as the line between art and sensationalism. Pulling off an outfit with authority is essential when you've chosen to resemble a cookie. Since I'm inherently cautious, I retreated to the understated and scrapped the belt.

I arrived at the museum to find friends, relatives, and prominent guests gathering at the entrance. After glancing at my invitation, a guard directed me to a large rectangular room displaying gravestone epitaphs on the walls and embroidered tapestry kneelers arranged in rows on the floor. The colorful kneelers, known as hassocks, were borrowed from English country churches and depicted family and local history. I'm sure they also did a great job supporting arthritic knees. Incidentally, pictorial narratives rendered in cross-stitch never adorned any midwestern church my family attended. Our childhood Sundays were spent kneeling on sticky beige vinyl. Whereas German houses of worship equate piety with misery. The faithful kneel on slender, unpadded boards in bone-chilling churches and sit on benches featuring backrest beams that dig into their shoulders, forcing them to sit up straight. Can people genuinely concentrate on the task at hand when shivering and uncomfortable?

Having spent a few minutes talking with friends, I wandered around the garden of kneelers and then took a second lap to focus on the walls. The epitaphs were witty, and among them, I discovered the perfect sentiment to sum up my life: *She did what she could.* My exit will be followed by cremation, therefore, I won't require a gravestone. Still, the aphorism could be woven into my eulogy. The exhibit got me thinking about death, and I wouldn't have been contemplating mortality had I stayed home and watched an episode of *The Crown.*

The satirical tongue-in-cheek gravestone epitaphs flaunted drumroll names like Winterbottom and Birdwhistle. School history lessons hammer away at battles, treaties, dates, and presidents, and we're lucky to remember any of them. On the other hand, the village parlance mirrors the times better than any classroom. One tombstone inscription revealed: *Thomas Thetcher died of a violent fever contracted by drinking a small beer when hot.* Small beer was the light beer of the eighteenth century and was vastly preferable to the contaminated drinking water available to most of the population. People went from breast to Budweiser without a drop of guilt and enjoyed a lifelong buzz of inebriation. Regrettably, Thetcher's cold, small beer was tainted. Fortunately, Benjamin Franklin's eighteenth-century breakfast beer was germ-free. Cheers to lightning rods and bifocals. Ben penned his own epitaph: *The body of B. Franklin, a printer, like the cover of an old book, its contents torn out and stripped of its lettering and gilding, lies here, food for worms.* Ben was a Founding Father of the United States and an accomplished author, political theorist, politician, Freemason, postmaster, scientist, inventor, humorist, civic activist, statesman, and diplomat. Nevertheless, he chose to immortalize himself as a printer. It doesn't get much more self-deprecating than that.

As far as the afterlife was concerned, grade school nuns assured me that the compass of my soul pointed upward while my body awaited salvation below. Still, I can't picture decomposing in a cemetery. The sky burial of Tibet is not my cup of yak butter tea either; the deceased are abandoned on a mountaintop to be eaten by birds. An even more terrifying tradition is the water burial of the Pacific islands, in which the corpse is sacrificed to sharks.

In the end, I will share my salvageable organs with the living, and the rest will be stored in a biodegradable cardboard urn depicting a sunset. Although I'm also considering a seashell fashioned from clay and cotton, which would dissolve in water and unite my remains with the ocean.

There's nothing like a day at a museum to stretch the boundaries of the imagination. It's true that not all art leaves an indelible impression, but neither does all food, and that has never stopped anyone from eating.

Public Places

Whenever I'm in a public place, I try to remain invisible. I don't eat smelly peanuts or crunchy apples. And I would never crack gum, jiggle my leg, or honk like a pink-footed goose when blowing my nose. If I don't make other people miserable, I hope they will reciprocate with like-minded politeness.

I dread flying, not because I'm concerned about crashing, but because I fear getting stuck beside an annoying person. One time, on a transatlantic flight, I sat next to a man with the physique of a woodsman. His left arm extended far into the space of my seventeen-inch seat, and to avoid brushing against him, I had to scoot toward the aisle, essentially inviting his limb to encroach even further. Sacrificing six inches of seat width on a long flight was more than I could bear. But what was I supposed to say? Why don't you try sitting with your arms jutting forward like a T-Rex? With each passing hour, my despair fermented into a sour mood.

Complaints often come across as assaults, and my rebuke would have dominated the atmosphere of the entire nine-hour flight. So, I said nothing. The man was oblivious to the fact that he was usurping my space, yet as not to offend him, I curled up like an armadillo. A while later, I took a futile jaunt around the plane searching for an empty seat, and then surrendered myself to the situation.

My misery reached an all-time high during dinner. Because of the man's broad wingspan, his elbow hovered above my tray, and a blond hair dangled from his shirt into my salad dressing. Finally, he left me no choice but to poke his arm with my plastic knife. At least, that's what I wanted to do.

Once upon a time, during a train ride from Munich to Vienna, I looked forward to five hours of uninterrupted reading. Ever ready for the worst, I brought my all-time favorite gadget: noise-canceling earbuds. The earbuds connect to a device that resembles a music player, but is really a white noise machine. It gives the impression that I'm listening to compressed music like most people on public transportation, but I'm actually enjoying the hiss of silence.

Upon boarding the train, I locate my seat, stow my backpack, and then sit down and assess my neighbors. Across the aisle, a toddler reclines in his mother's arms, and her kindergarten-age brother sits quietly beside the father in the row behind them. The family chats softly while passing a container of sliced fruit back and forth. Astonished by my good fortune, I dare open my book.

After thirty minutes, my world changes forever. The toddler climbs onto his mother's lap and cries out, "Hoppy, Hoppy Rider!" The mommy is more than willing to entertain her progeny and trumpets the popular German nursery rhyme while bouncing the toddler, now squealing with delight, on her knee.

Roughly translated, the verse goes like this: *Bumpety bump, rider. When he falls, he howls. If he falls into the pond, nobody will find him. If he falls into the ditch, the ravens will eat him. If he falls into the swamp, he goes splash!* The mother's legs fly open, and the child lurches toward the floor, shrieking even louder. Inevitably, he wants more. So she repeats the schtick at least ten more times. Then, unexpectedly, the older child leaps up and begs to be bumpetied. I turn up the volume on my white noise machine and grit my teeth, minus the protection of my high-priced mouth guard.

I have kids, but I would feel impertinent winding them up in public. Wouldn't it be nice if people occupied public spaces instead of invading them? There's a time and a place for everything. What would travelers say if I played my clarinet in the aisle?

Sometimes, a crisis can't be avoided, like when a child has a temper tantrum. I sympathize with the perpetrator as long as he is under four. A tantrum is a human attribute without an off switch. Your sweetie pie will morph from cute and cuddly to whiny and demanding faster than you can blink.

Then, without warning, the angelic recipient of your DNA becomes deaf and begins to wail and flail on the floor. In most cases, people recognize your helplessness and spare you further humiliation by staring straight ahead.

One year, we took our daughter to a Japanese restaurant for her birthday. We expected a peaceful evening of buttery raw fish and pleasant conversation. Instead, we got a loud-mouthed business executive romanticizing his job, patronizing his friends, and magnifying his importance in a voice reminiscent of a gnu. Is he expecting applause? Shall we pat the great dealmaker's swollen head on our way out? A frosty glance in his direction did nothing to lessen his boasting.

I recently met a friend for coffee in a bustling café and watched her scroll through her phone while we waited for our server. As my friend was too busy to talk, I eavesdropped on the surrounding chitchat. And then I thought, did I really take time out of my day to listen to the maladies of strangers? After we placed our order, her phone remained on the table.

"I guess it doesn't want coffee. Maybe a plug?"

"Oh, sorry," she said, "I'm expecting an important message. Do you mind?"

Nah, I'll grab my Kindle and read a bit because I have important things to read today.

Steve Jobs once said that the 'i' in Apple products stands for internet, individual, instruct, inform, and inspire. But, he forgot, intrusive, inconsiderate, and impolite. An hour into our visit, I realized I couldn't compete with such a captivating playmate. It was impossible for my friend not to glance at her screen every few seconds. Is that a healthy relationship, or is it bondage?

That night, I googled phone addiction, and the term for that is nomophobia, fear of being without a mobile phone. The only thing I'm afraid of being without is my wits.

The key to public behavior lies in the awareness of your potential to offend others. My aim is to act like a *Homo sapien*. It means wise man in Latin.

It's That Time of Year

After a lifetime of filing taxes, the procedure still makes me uptight. It's not the tedium of the forms I abhor, but the fear of miscalculation. Churches forgive incompetence, but governments punish it. Every year, the season of blooming flowers and hatchlings is marred by tax returns. Most people just shake their heads and file, although I have a friend who doesn't believe in paying taxes, which is why he doesn't. Recently, I asked him about it.

"Look, Melvin, since you don't intend to pay taxes, you'll have to pitch a tent in the wilderness and live off the land. Utility services won't be necessary because you'll be slurping from an idyllic river, assuming a bloated deer carcass isn't contaminating the water. You'll have to risk food-borne illness because hunting and gathering will be your supermarket, and the FDA will not be there to inspect your victuals. On the plus side, those raspberries and trout are free. The government didn't put them there, so help yourself. Just make sure you're not camping in a national park because Uncle Sam maintains that neck of the woods."

Melvin rolled his eyes. "I'm not gonna go to work every day and pay a portion of my hard-earned dollars to the government. They're just giving it to people who don't want to work."

"Granted, poverty is a losing battle for some. And yes, welfare should be a lifeboat, not a cruise ship. But, sadly, abuse of the system is inevitable. Honestly, I understand your frustration. Fraudulent practices permeate every society. People aren't supposed to buy cigarettes with food stamps, but it happens. And bankers shouldn't launder drug cartel money, but yeah, they do, and since they look respectable, we end up bailing them out."

He shook his head. "When I was a kid, my parents paid for me to attend a private school, yet they still had to fork over taxes for public schools. You think that's okay?"

"Well, Mel, unless you cruised to the classroom on a flying carpet, your school bus traveled on publicly funded roads. It turns out that your new lifestyle will not require infrastructures, such as roads, bridges, airports, or the post office. Your quest for self-reliance is admirable."

"I'm already paying sales tax on everything I buy. Plus, the wealthy don't pay their fair share. They know all the loopholes. And besides, filing is way too complicated!"

"True, taxation needs to be reformed. It would be great if we had a fair yet simple tax system, but I'm not holding my breath. I'm also not admitting defeat, but face it, Melvin, human beings are flawed, and they are the ones running the show. Consider the following scenario. A killer breaks out of jail and hides out in the wilderness near your tent. Your no-tax doctrine means no cops. They won't work for fish and berries, so if the slasher messes with you, then what? Now that I think about it, there wouldn't be any jails, and criminals would run rampant. Not to mention, it might be a good idea to extinguish your cigarette because city hall pays the firefighters."

"Okay, let's say I decide to rough it in the woods. I don't need garbage pickup, and I'm not polluting the air with a car. What do you have to say to that?"

"You want a pat on the back? What if a million other disgruntled tax abstainers joined you? Too much poo in the forest would not be amusing, and you'd probably end up with cholera. Remember, you served in the military. Now, who do you think bankrolled your paycheck? By the way, the price of one fighter jet could fund the arts for a year. And since the arts are already hanging by a cliff, maybe you could talk to your buddies and ask them whether they might sacrifice a new plane on behalf of music, painting, and ballet."

"Why should we patronize the arts? The government is already too big, and I don't want to pay for all that unnecessary stuff."

"Melvin, sometimes you can be such a simpleton. Do you know what Charles de Gaul once said? How can anyone govern a nation with two hundred and forty-six kinds of cheese?"

"I don't parlez vous, so what are you trying to say?"

"Every person has different needs. We have to accept the fact that our causes are diverse yet equally relevant, and there will always be spending that we consider wasteful. If you're feeling gloomy next April, remember the grass is not always greener on the other side. Sales tax in the European Union averages twenty percent, and Belgians pay forty-two percent of their wages to the government. You can buy three gallons of gas in the US for the price of one in Europe."

"I don't care about them. I care about me."

"Then maybe you can revolt creatively. For example, did you know that one of the most memorable tax protests occurred in the eleventh century?"

"This better be good."

"Oh, I promise you, it is. An English nobleman imposed excessive taxes on his subjects and ignored their ensuing hardship. Finally, his wife, Lady Godiva, took action."

"Lady Gaga lived a thousand years ago?"

"Melvin, please pay attention. Lady Godiva was distressed by the plight of the people and pleaded with her husband to lower the crippling tax."

"Sure, if you ride naked through the streets of Coventry," he snickered.

"His wife disrobed, mounted her horse, and paraded down Main street au naturel. Her curtain of long hair spared her dignity, and Godiva's husband winced but kept his promise and revoked the despised tax. History winked at justice."

"You want me to wink at justice?"

"Melvin, I want you to jump in the lake."

103

Planet Jackpot

My husband and I often enjoy a morning stroll through the woods at the end of our street. The trees form a leafy cathedral bursting with life, and losing them to a chainsaw is unimaginable. You would think that people inherently appreciate trees, but the trouble is that many don't. For example, our neighbor despises the chestnut in our backyard. We planted the tree when our son was born and are emotionally attached to every inch. It grows six feet from the property boundary line and has been trimmed by a certified arborist. Yet the guy gripes incessantly about the shade our tree casts on his grassless lot, which is strewn with gravel and cluttered with junk. Not only is his property an eyesore, but his shabby garage sprouts a whopper of an antenna and a satellite dish. A faded poster has been peeling off the garage door for the twenty-four years we have lived here.

Be that as it may, there is one beautiful object our neighbor can gaze upon while crunching around his backyard, and that is our tree. For months now, Herr von Grumpy has been on the rampage because we have refused to cut the tree to his liking, meaning down to a stump. In all seriousness, he told us he hired a company to trim the tree from his side of the property line. After he informed us of this ludicrous plan, my body had an all-out visceral reaction. Bolstered by a hammering heart, quaking limbs, and constricted breath, I hissed at him, "If you do that, I will call the police."

To which he replied, "Your tree shades my yard." Actually, he repeated the sentence several times like a mantra.

"That's what trees do. By law, and I looked this up, they are permitted to create shade. Although you could look at it this way; our tree provides shade."

At that moment, I had an epiphany. I looked at our neighbor, our shared disdain brewing, and said to him, "You hate our tree."

"I don't hate your tree," he said and stormed off.

But that was the crux of the issue. I realized there are tree enthusiasts, like us, tree bystanders who don't care much either way, and loggers who regard trees as lumber. Then there are the biophobics who harbor a genuine aversion to trees. So, I suspect our neighbor will have to live in misery as long as our innocent, lovely tree blows in the wind. And do you know how long that will be? Until our ashes are fertilizing its hungry roots. Sorry, Jesus, but I cannot love my neighbor as I love myself.

And when I go inside to escape the neighbor, I have a second epiphany. I may adore trees, but I am also an accomplice in their demise. I turn on the television and watch the sickening reality of forests being razed to provide land for cash crops, such as my morning coffee, grown on a plantation in the ravaged soil of a massacre. So why, I wonder, have I not been buying fair trade beans? It's not like I'll be lunching in a soup kitchen if I indulge in sustainable coffee beans. Fair trade farmers grow coffee and cocoa next to native plants. Their crops flourish in the shade of the rainforest, and they merely need longer to mature than their plantation siblings.

The fact is, I've played a more significant role than I ever imagined in harming our natural world. Last week, a sea turtle choked on my supermarket shopping bag, believing it to be a jellyfish. My plastic yogurt cup ended up in the stomach of a whale. The yogurt was organic, the container not so much. I produce a constant drizzle of trash, and it really adds up. Fortunately, my plastic refuse gets picked up and hauled to a recycling plant every two weeks. The shampoo bottle of today is the traffic cone of tomorrow, right? In some cases, yes. Plastic waste is a considerable export commodity and often gets shipped to poor countries for recycling. But, oops, once in a while, it slips into the ocean.

Ecosystems are collapsing faster than we can eat a bar of chocolate. Millions of acres of victorious soy, coffee, and palm oil chisel away our wilderness, forcing homeless wildlife into smaller habitats where pathogens run amok. Earth's creatures are reciprocal and don't hesitate to pass their ailments on to us. Coronavirus comes to mind. As crazy as it may sound, the vampire bats of Brazil have begun sucking on human necks since we wiped out the birds they usually feed on. I'm not surprised that the Earth is baring its teeth, "You're eliminating yourselves, and once you're gone, I will recover," the planet chuckles.

It turns out that our interlocking ecological system, better known as the food chain, is also out of whack. If bees die out, and it looks like they are doing just that, the sex lives of plants will take a turn for the worse. We better get used to tortilla chips without guacamole and margaritas sans lime juice. Half of our fruits and vegetables rely on these super pollinators, and their extinction would trigger a domino effect, including the death of the plants they fertilize.

For years, I've anesthetized myself from the facts. Eighty percent of the world's forests have already been destroyed, and soon, we will inhabit a planet with more plastic in the oceans than fish. Isn't their fate our fate? Aren't we woven into the fabric of every plant and animal on the planet? Climate change is as old as the Earth, but fluctuations that once occurred every few thousand years transpire in mere decades. I live in Bavaria, and the weather seesaws like the moods of a pubescent teenager. Still, there's something bizarre about balmy beer garden weather in January and snowstorms in May.

One year, my parents stuffed their five kids into a beat-up station wagon for a trip out west. I remember folding down the rear seats and transforming the car into a playground.

Our luggage was belted to the roof, but we, on the other hand, were untethered. Seatbelts were not fashionable in the seventies. Four days after leaving Ohio, we stopped in Vegas, which was disappointingly crummy. The real jackpot was down the road at Lake Mead. Turquoise-hued water made us dizzy with desire, and the wild surroundings added to our dreamlike bliss. We swam among fish as long as our legs. I remember being stunned not so much by the size of the fish but by the fact that I could actually see them. The water was nothing like murky Lake Erie where I usually swam.

Thirty years later, my husband and I took our kids to Lake Mead and peered inside a dried-up basin. Imposing bathtub rings taunted my childhood memory. Take another big gulp, Vegas. By no means is it outrageous to expect New England lawns and lengthy showers in the middle of the desert.

When my mother was a child, meat was consumed on Sundays. My grandfather slaughtered a chicken behind the garage, and my grandmother plucked it in the kitchen. Food was fast before it was dead, not after. Nowadays, packaged, processed, frozen, additive-filled fake food often rules the roost. McNightmare has ripped a hole in European cuisine, and I'm surprised by its popularity, considering Europeans are pretty emotional about food, especially bread. Although, I've never seen a cheeseburger clamped under the armpit of a cycling Frenchman. Our European ancestors didn't throw away stale bread; they used it to make dumplings. These days, factories produce bread dumplings wrapped in boil bags that look like tennis balls. The convenience is irresistible. Pass the mashed potato flakes, please.

One day, I asked Alexa how to fix the planet. Before she could answer, that girl of all trades, Siri, chimed in and said we should drive less and walk more because she is sick and tired of traffic questions. Not to be outdone, Alexa replied, "Feel free to bring reusable bags to the grocery store. By the way, there's a great selection marked down on Amazon."

Siri jumped in, "While you're at it, add a weed puller to the cart and skip the herbicides."

"I echo that," replied Alexa.

We are leading the world with our ingenuity. Just ask the two most intelligent girls on the planet. Ecology and industry can coexist. Perhaps former coal miners could build solar parks. Who's telling us it's jobs or the environment? The Earth doesn't belong to a political party. Planet Jackpot belongs to us and is the most significant inheritance we will ever receive. Just ask Siri.

Peek a Boohoo

I was drinking coffee in the kitchen when a deluge of inaudible insects appeared out of nowhere. No matter how many times I blinked, they refused to disappear. Fruit flies fornicating in the bananas again, I thought. As soon as my husband came home, I pulled him into the room.

"Do you see any bugs in here?"

He looked around and said, "No."

"That's it, just no."

"No, nothing's bugging me."

"Very funny. They've been tormenting me for an hour. Something is wrong with my eyes, and it's after office hours."

When your body inflicts a symptom upon you, it's either an inconvenience, like a headache, or a warning, such as impending blindness.

"We should go to the emergency room."

"Gashes and broken bones are unquestionably issues for the emergency room, but flies in the eyes?"

He pulled out his phone, and in less than a minute, we had the address of an eye clinic in downtown Munich.

"I bet this will take half the night," I moaned.

We encountered heavy traffic driving into the city but found parking immediately. When we got out of the car, my husband held his phone like a divining rod and searched for the clinic. After a few minutes, he stopped in front of a run-down building. "Here we are," he said.

"Are you kidding me?" I yelped. "I have never seen such a decrepit-looking hospital."

We entered the building, and needless to say, the interior was even worse. I was shocked to find a dirty floor and shabby furniture. The war-torn look was more than unsettling. Aren't hospitals supposed to have that bleachy feeling?

I registered at the beat-up front desk and joined my husband in the crowded waiting room. Looking around, I thought my co-waiters looked somewhat bedraggled; on second thought, who dresses up for an accident? Once, I nearly severed a finger pruning a bouquet with poultry shears, and I certainly did not brush my hair or change my clothes before heading to the emergency room. Besides, a blood-soaked shirt screams me first.

We passed the time googling eye disorders on our phones. Never before had I traversed the ocular landscape, and it was nothing less than captivating.

An hour later, a nurse called my name and escorted me to an examination room. Typing away on the computer was a young doctor. How do you judge the caliber of an unfamiliar doctor? Old age implies experience, and youngish connotes technological proficiency. But in the end, desperation has the upper hand.

Imagine how Bach must have felt when a surgeon with filthy hands jabbed an unhygienic instrument into his eyes without anesthesia. Naturally, the composer trusted the doctor to repair his vision, and I suppose the surgeon had faith in Bach to compose a superb cantata for Sunday's service. Albeit, thanks to him, as a blind man.

The doctor interrupted my reverie. "I must dilate your eyes to examine the retina. The process takes around thirty minutes." He put drops in my eyes and sent me back to the waiting room. Now and then, a tired-looking nurse administered more.

After my world was sufficiently blurry, I returned to the examination room. The doctor sat behind an eye scope and said, "Place your chin on the tissue paper and press your forehead into the band." Then he instructed me to look up, down, and all around. Next, he filled an ocular cup with gel and suctioned it to my eye. I pretended not to mind.

"There's a hole in your retina," he said. "I'll have to seal it with a laser. This procedure takes place down the hall. Please follow me."

Before playing *Star Wars* inside my eyeball, Dr. Skywalker brightened my day with numbing drops. The laser didn't inflict a yelping kind of pain, but more of a tolerable ache. I wondered why looking at a laser pointer could blind me, but being lasered would save my sight.

The following afternoon, while washing my hands, black and reddish swirls billowed like clouds across the sink. A moment later, blood gushed painlessly into my field of vision and turned my vitreous humor into a strawberry daiquiri. During my wait at the clinic the previous evening, I became familiar with terms such as vitreous, which is the transparent gelatinous substance that gives your eyes their spherical shape and fills the space between the lens and retina.

My hands trembled as I dialed our local eye doctor. The receptionist told me to come in as soon as possible, and since driving was out of the question, I rushed to catch the next train. Fortunately, the practice was only two stops away.

When I entered the doctor's office, a nurse immediately ushered me into a room, covered my good eye, and asked me to read the chart.

"What chart?"

She sat down and rolled up to me on a swiveling stool with casters. Her knees briefly bumped mine.

"Can you read this?"

"Sorry, but I don't see anything." She fanned my face with the card. "Now, what do you see?"

I removed the patch from my good eye. "I see one Big E."

The doctor arrived and examined my eye. "You've had a vitreous hemorrhage, and your retina may be detaching. We cannot tell for sure because the blood in your vitreous humor is obstructing our view. You'll have to go downtown to the eye clinic."

His receptionist gave me the address of an unfamiliar clinic, and I returned to the subway station. After boarding the train, I sat down and wept. Did you know that pressing your tongue against the roof of your mouth will stop you from crying. Biting your tongue is another method, but why add insult to injury. Across from me, a woman pretended to read a book. Once I got a hold of myself, I satisfied her need to know and called my husband. He answered on the second ring.

"My right eye filled with blood this afternoon. I saw our eye doctor, who recommended I go to an eye hospital in Munich. It's not where we were last night. I'm completely bl...," I simply could not say the word. "I can't see out of my right eye," I sobbed. "I'm on the train to Munich."

"And I'm heading home. I'll turn around at the next stop and meet you at the hospital."

"There's nothing you can do. Just go home, and I'll call you when I know more. By the way, there's soup on the stove."

After arriving at the clinic, I underwent a variety of tests. A doctor evaluated the results and said, "I want you to go home, sleep upright, and return to the hospital tomorrow morning. You need surgery."

Maybe horses and flamingos can sleep upright, but not me. I spent the night making trips to the bathroom to see whether the blood had been magically reabsorbed. The following day, I returned to the clinic, and unlike last night's doctor, today's doctor was confident that an operation wasn't necessary.

"We'll just wait and see whether the blood goes away on its own. Based on your tests, there doesn't seem to be a retinal tear."

"Wait and see sounds like a good idea, but what if it's wait and not see? I have a flight booked to the States next week. Is it safe for me to fly?"

"That shouldn't be a problem."

First of all, he didn't thwart my travel plans, and he said I wouldn't need surgery. Therefore, I had no cause to doubt his judgment; he told me exactly what I wanted to hear.

"By the way, how long does it usually take for the blood to dissipate?"

"Two to three months."

"Months, really?"

"Yes, months."

Eye doctors are remarkably succinct.

Somewhat apprehensively, I boarded the flight to Texas. The purpose of the trip was to visit my siblings and scatter my father's ashes.

During my stay, I lived with my sister Stacey. Shortly after my arrival, we met the rest of the family on my brother's boat. Dad rode in his urn; well, some of him did. My sister gave each of us a portion of his ashes, which I keep in a box on my nightstand.

Our private tribute embodied who he was: an informal, humorous, and warm-hearted man. I would never bury him, so it made little difference how or where his funeral was held. We eulogized him, and his life unfolded and floated over the lake. He was a drummer, and if ashes could talk, he might have said, "I'm happy you could all make it to my final gig."

Several days later, a foreboding black disk rose like an evil sun from the bottom of my eye. I turned to Stacey and said, "It looks like a fountain pen broke inside my head. Do you have a decent ophthalmologist?"

"As a matter of fact, I do."

We called the doctor and explained the situation. He said, "Your retina is detaching, which means it is pulling away from your eye like a sheet of wallpaper. Come to my office at eight tomorrow morning."

Retinas don't have nerve endings; consequently, when this layer of tissue, which belongs to the brain, is failing, there's no physical suffering nudging you to see a doctor. In most cases, flashing lights and, as I recently discovered, swarms of insects indicate retinal holes, but the bloody cocktail inside my eye obscured the signs.

The next day, the ophthalmologist examined my eye. "You must have a vitrectomy within twenty-four hours to preserve your vision. During surgery, we will replace the vitreous with a bubble of gas. For the first two weeks after surgery, you must face the floor. This is called face-down posturing. The position of your head will push the gas bubble against the retina until it heals. Additionally, you cannot fly for a month. The high altitude would cause the gas to expand and irreparably damage your eye."

"But I have a flight home next week."

"Not anymore."

His secretary provided me with a brochure describing the procedure and postoperative care. When we got home, I opened the pamphlet and was shocked to see a picture of a woman nestled in what appeared to be a fitness machine. The headline read: *Vitrectomy Recovery Equipment Rental.*

I showed it to my sister. "What's this for?"

"I don't know."

I continued reading, and all I can say is drum roll, please, for the face-down support system. The equipment would help me maintain this position without strain. Regardless, I chose to forgo the contraption.

Before long, crumbs and dust bunnies would be my world. May I invite you to contemplate the hair in the tub with me. My brooding was interrupted by the phone. It was the doctor's office, "I'm sorry, we can't operate until you pay for the surgery. I need your credit card information."

I read her the slew of numbers and wondered what people without seventeen hundred dollars in spare cash were supposed to do, visit the white cane shop?

Early the next morning, we drove to the hospital. Once again, my credit card was requested.

"Oh, I paid last night," I said.

"You paid the doctor, and now you must pay the hospital. That will be twenty-five hundred dollars."

"I'm here for outpatient surgery, so it can't be that expensive."

"No, twenty-five hundred is the correct amount."

I handed over my card, and the machine rejected it. My black frisbee took a little spin.

"You're over your limit."

My sister kindly lent me her card. Low credit limits may be frustrating, but they shouldn't have the power to make you blind. Since I was insured in Germany, the bills had to be paid upfront and submitted to the company for reimbursement.

A nurse escorted me to a curtained cubicle, where I changed into a fetching hospital gown. After giving a few vials of blood, I received an injection of pre-op medicine that lifted my spirits and made me chatty.

Several hours later, I found myself sitting in the back seat of my sister's car, wearing an eye patch and clutching gigantic sunglasses. A bag containing drops, pills, and a hard shell patch rested in my lap. I don't remember getting into the car, and I don't recall getting dressed. Yet, I remembered to look down, which was easy since I was still drowsy, and the sunlight was intense enough to irritate even my unimpaired eye.

Fortunately, I usually sleep on my stomach. But how was I supposed to sleep with my face buried in the pillow? The doctor was adamant, face down means face down. So, I positioned my body diagonally across the bed and dangled my head over the edge. My functioning eye hovered above the chair beside the bed, and my Kindle rested on its cushion. I took comfort in the fuzzy, illuminated words.

A few days later, Stacey put a flat-screen TV on the floor at the foot of the bed. Face-down posturing people can't possibly trip over objects on the floor; this hazard exists only for the un-vitrectomied.

I felt like the hands of a clock rotating around a bed of entertainment. There was a dachshund (an actual animal) on my pillow, a book at my side, and a television at my feet.

My sister walked me and the dog every day. Strolling down the street with my head bowed, I resembled a disgraced pet who had just laid waste to the muffins cooling on the table. Let the neighbors' imaginations run wild, I thought. Wheel-chairs, crutches, and neck braces show that you've been in-jured. Poor you requires a mobility aid or a brace because you are healing and suffering. Onlookers feel compassion. On the other hand, walking with your head down implies that you are mentally challenged or have lost a contact lens. Honestly, who has ever heard of a vitrectomy and the operation's bizarre posturing? Not even my spell checker recognizes the word — vasectomy, anyone.

One day, my brother took me to the supermarket. Walking alongside him, I was amazed to discover various products on the bottom shelves I had never noticed before. When we arrived at the produce section, I said, "I'm slowing you down. Just park me here and pick me up when you're ready to check out."

I stood like a statue next to the melons and stared at the scuffed linoleum. Children were understandably curious. "What's wrong with her, Daddy?" they stage whispered. I'm not deaf, little girl, but I'm going to pretend that I am so I can hear what y'all are saying about me. The kids who said,

"I wonder what she has," realized an illness had afflicted me. Those who asked, "What's wrong with her?" insinuated that this flaw was my choice. Yesiree, Bob, I love staring at my feet sixteen hours a day because I have not yet found a therapist who can fix me. By the way, you are wearing ugly shoes. I should have put an empty berry box on the ground and collected coins like a Florentine street mime. I wish I could have borrowed the PA system. I would have announced, "Hear ye, hear ye shoppers, delicious cantaloupes are half-price today. By the way, the woman standing beside the fruit is staring at the ground because of an eye operation. Be careful, she bites."

During a follow-up appointment at the surgeon's office in San Antonio, I complained to a nurse about the gas bubble squelching my flight back to Germany. Her answer was truly painful; she suggested I drive.

Time flies as fast as a barn owl when your only purpose in life is inspecting the floor. Eventually, the day arrived for me to return home. My eye didn't explode while crossing the Atlantic, but I noticed that my vision was becoming foggy. I wasn't alarmed because the doctor in Texas had informed me that vitrectomies can cause cataracts. However, the ensuing cataract surgery unexpectedly resulted in a corneal erosion. I bet you never gave a second thought to your cornea. It's the transparent part of the eye covering your pupil. Take a bow cornea, you are responsible for two-thirds of the eye's focusing ability. When that itty bitty window is broken, it is unbelievably painful, and you will spend gobs of money on drops and ointments.

I reimbursed my sister and looked forward to my insurance company squaring up the bill. Instead, they said, "You may recall the letter we sent you a few months ago informing you that, as of now, your coverage is limited to the European Union."

Well, they absolutely didn't say it like that. Tedious legal jargon garnished with Latin made me toss it. Oh, how vitreous unhumorous.

Introducing the Kitchen

I was dusting our downstairs guest room, and in a flash of clarity, I realized the space would make an ideal kitchen. We are dreadfully cramped in our current kitchen, and I wondered why I hadn't considered this sooner. In addition to being larger and brighter, this room has two windows looking out onto the garden. Should the idea be feasible, we could stand at the window sipping coffee while watching the neighbor's cat gaze longingly at our goldfish pond. So, switching rooms made perfect sense.

That evening, after considerable deliberation, my husband agreed to the transformation and was just as enthusiastic. We were swept up in a powerful current of determination and asked a handyman to evaluate the situation.

"We'd need to cut a hole in the floor to access the basement plumbing, but there's no reason why this room can't be converted into a kitchen," he assured us.

Whenever friends visited, they did not hesitate to explore the possibilities. "Why don't you knock down a few walls and open up the downstairs?"

"Having separate rooms is practical, and since we're musicians, we want to confine the sound. We practice something precisely because it sounds bad, and nobody wants to listen to that."

Almost every week, we browsed around a kitchen store. The selection was as stunning as the prices were shocking. Modern kitchens are works of art, and appliances are not just conveniences anymore. They are high-tech marvels. The diversity of countertops alone was mind-blowing. There was the laminate of my childhood, granite, germ-resistant stainless steel, veined marble that would have made Michelangelo drool, pricey soapstone, slate, reclaimed wood, recycled aluminum, and our favorite, the ceramic slab. Archeologists have been unearthing ceramics dating as far back as twenty-nine thousand BC. So, it stands to reason that this countertop would last a lifetime and be around for future generations as well.

On a rainy Saturday morning, we visited a furniture store featuring a sprawling kitchen showroom. A competent saleswoman led us around multiple exhibits explaining the pros and cons of various cabinet fronts, drawers, sinks, and backsplashes. After months of searching, we finally discovered a retailer whose products and prices were in sync. Also, we found the ideal kitchen. Light gray ceramic cabinets paired with a textured ceramic countertop and a milky white glass backsplash begged to come home with us. It was all very minimalistic, which means easy to clean in my book.

Our kitchen guru also recommended an oven, stovetop, dishwasher, and refrigerator. Since she was clearly an authority on appliances, we accepted her suggestions. Then, she offered to design the kitchen right then and there. I handed her a rough sketch of the room, including its dimensions, and after looking it over, she said, "I can work with this, but our installers will come out and take exact measurements. Feel free to wander around the store for an hour while I plan your kitchen."

Nike was the Greek goddess of speed, and like they say, if the shoe fits... The next thing I knew, we were at her desk admiring our new kitchen on a monitor the size of a bathtub. "Have a seat," she said. Then, she gave us a digital tour of our soon-to-be cooking utopia. We applauded her ingenuity and shoved our credit card into the machine for the down payment.

Two months later, a kitchen that cost as much as my parents' first house was delivered and installed by two skilled workers. We were eager to fill the cabinets and try out the appliances equipped with artificial intelligence. Artificial being the drawback. At first, our smart gadgets were impressive, but it soon became apparent that they had minds of their own. For instance, when you want to open our dishwasher, all you have to do is nudge its handleless door. But it also opens its mouth when you wipe its front panel. Evidently, the machine can't distinguish between an intentional push, a wipe, or an accidental bump. And, when I close the door, half the time, it pops open. Why? Is our little control freak craving some fresh air? I've tried prodding it shut to no avail. Slamming makes it burst open with a vengeance. A dishwasher should simplify my life, not make my colon spastic.

Another frustrating feature is the sensor that starts the wash cycle. In case you didn't know, sensors are as moody as teenagers; they respond when they feel like it. My question is, how can I turn you on dishwasher? Am I using too much or too little pressure? Is your sensor wet? I never imagined that I would need the advice of a scientist to operate a kitchen appliance. Yet I did. I called my physicist son and whined about the misbehaving machine. He said, "The sensor is not wet, it's dirty. Just clean it."

Although the dishwasher has an impressive feature, it beams expendable information onto the floor, informing me whether it is scrubbing, rinsing, or drying. Finally, I know what's going on in there.

Some cooks are induction aficionados. Not me. My state-of-the-art induction burners give me a magnetic wave of frustration. Only cookware with a high ferrous metal content will react with the burner and generate heat. If you are un-sure whether a pot is compatible with your finicky appliance, grab a refrigerator magnet and see whether it adheres to the bottom. If it does, your cookware and induction stovetop will get along. I had to say goodbye to all my pots and pans, including my practical spaghetti pot with the built-in strainer basket. I'm not averse to the stovetop, but I could easily live without its eccentricities. A concert of humming and buzzing accompanies the more traditional simmering and sizzling.

The stovetop dislikes getting wet, more so than our dog. And unlike our spaniel, who simply looks pitiful when wet, the stovetop is vocal about it. When I lift a lid and condensed water hits the surface, it emits a series of beeps. Wiping the water with my dishrag only spreads the moisture and escalates the dinging. When water boils over, all hell breaks loose, and the stovetop sends out mayday signals before shutting down.

Despite everything, I try to appreciate its qualities. Induction stovetops are energy efficient. Bravo. And they only heat the space your cookware occupies. Plus, they cook more rapidly. But you should not get within two feet of the stovetop should you have a pacemaker because the electromagnetic field can interfere with your device. Kitchen gadgets ought to improve life and not threaten it. Then again, I can leave a dish towel on the stove, and it will not catch fire.

I'm never uptight when operating the new microwave. I put a cold plate of lasagna inside the appliance, touch the sensor, and electromagnetic radio waves warm up my dinner. The sensor is not discriminating; it even responds to wet, sticky fingers. My microwave is simple to use and easy to clean. Once, I forgot to cover the lasagna, and exploding tomato sauce made the inside look like a crime scene. Still, the microwave didn't go haywire beeping about it.

I have a friend who refuses to buy a microwave because she believes it emits dangerous radiation. True, but those waves are contained in a robust metal box that does not allow them to escape. Many hazardous machines come with sturdy metal boxes, like your car's engine. You wouldn't open the hood and put your Chihuahua inside to dry off, so why have people used microwaves to dry their pets? That kind of behavior gives microwave ovens a bad rap. I don't know anything about physics, but I know microwaves are used in cell phones, and nobody seems to mind holding those next to their brains.

My favorite appliance is our new pyrolitic oven, which means it cleans itself. We should have a public holiday for the person who invented this feature. Scorched sauce, burnt cheese, and a buildup of unidentifiable grime and grease make the oven one of the most despicable household items to clean. While holding my breath, I sprayed our former oven with noxious foam, then stuck my head inside to scrub the filthy wire scaffolding, as well as every nook and cranny. I detested the whole sordid business.

How about a round of applause for the self-cleaning oven, the unrivaled king of the kitchen. I just wish designers would wake up and smell the latte; we need machines that are genuinely better and not just smarter.

Bon Appétit

Barefoot children dressed in second-hand clothing sit cross-legged on the floor, waiting. Women wrapped in saris place metal trays heaped with rice and dal, India's classic dish of spicy lentils, in front of them. Colorful vegetables garnish the mound, and little hands swipe with relish at the familiar meal. What's going on here? This food looks and smells fantastic. I peer inside the kitchen. Unbelievably, lunch was cooked on two hot plates connected to a rusty gas cylinder. Aside from the burners, there's an aluminum sink and a rickety table for preparing meals. Dumbfounded, I stand in the orphanage's hallway and watch my future daughter scoop fistfuls of the delectable concoction into her mouth. India not only thrives on this nutritious, cheap, and easy-to-prepare food, they are crazy about it.

Nothing in this place comes in plastic. Rice and lentils are delivered in burlap sacks, and vegetables arrive in wooden crates. These children forgo cookies, chips, and sugary drinks since anything packaged is beyond affordable. I suspect you could feed the entire orphanage for the price of a box of cupcakes. My daughter wasn't even aware that jellybeans existed until she was five years old. Her childhood beans grew on plants and were not delivered by a seasonal rabbit.

There is no dessert after lunch. Instead, warm cups of peanuts with tiny spoons are handed out in the afternoon. Peanuts seem like the ultimate finger food, and I wondered why they required cutlery when the hot, sticky lentils did not. Walking through the village that morning, I spotted a vendor selling banana slices pierced with toothpicks. Usually, I bite chunks from the partially peeled fruit, but now that I think about it, eating a banana that way doesn't look very sophisticated.

When did our nourishment become corroded? It must have regressed gradually, like a rusting car. Packaged, processed foods are convenient and bursting with artificial flavors that ambush our willpower. I worked at a fast-food joint when I was a teenager, and I'm sorry to say that frozen, pre-cooked ingredients and sauces stored in ten-gallon plastic tubs were the building blocks of the meal.

And then there's that intoxicating indulgence, sugar. Strawberries are delicious, but would I choose them over a double caramel, chocolate-covered ice cream bar. Probably not. I used to tell myself that dessert fed my sugar-loving brain. Then I read that brains only like glucose, not sucrose, better known as crystallized white sugar. All my life, it has snowed sugar, and yes, I know that empty calories invariably lead to weight gain and malnutrition. Even so, pleasure impedes my judgment. Sure, India has fast food, but a street food vendor whips up his goodies using fresh vegetables and legumes. It's common to find the cook flanked by bowls of rice and spices that were probably ground that morning.

Are the children in my daughter's orphanage spoiled? You bet. Fresh, wholesome, homemade food is all they know. Cookie jars and cupboards overflowing with mouthwatering snacks are confined to fantasy land. There is no such thing as out-of-control binging since the kids eat only what they are given. Do they miss junk food? Perhaps, but how can they miss something they've never had?

After my daughter arrived in Germany, I didn't want to pollute her taste buds; still, I wished to introduce her to the pleasure of chocolate. "Here you go, sweety, try this yummy candy. Look what you've been missing." I was sure she would scarf it down and beg for more. All kids want candy, right? No, they don't. She didn't inhale it. She took a cautious bite and said, "No like." Soft drinks garnered the same reaction. Fourteen years later, she still dislikes chocolate and cola. Her nighttime snack is usually a second helping of whatever we had for dinner. Yeah, she adores cheesecake as long as it's made in our kitchen. But her fondness for rice, white basmati rice, is unprecedented. Rice is high on the glycemic index, cry the experts. All the same, Asians are some of the oldest people on the planet. My Japanese mother-in-law is nearly ninety, and do you know what accompanies her glycemic health hazard:

fish, seaweed, and little fermented sour plums. She dips everything in soy sauce and a dollop of green horseradish paste, also known as wasabi.

On the flip side, bread screams for butter, cheese, and lunch meat. Don't forget the mayonnaise. Copious carbohydrates and nuggets fried in corn oil define our sustenance. Bodily organs that escape destruction by high cholesterol are knocked out by our exuberant ingestion of corn syrup. Oh, so sweet and inexpensive. It's in nearly everything that comes in a bottle, bag, box, or carton. That multi-talented sweetener and its sibling, glucose-fructose syrup, have hijacked our self-control.

I know many people don't have time to cook because they're swamped with work. Meanwhile, the women running the orphanage must have more time on their hands than we do. For instance, they never have to clean the bathtub, well, because there isn't one. Instead, bathing is performed with a cup and a bucket of water warmed by a portable heating rod. Here's how it works. The master of ceremonies dips the cup into the pail, pours water over a child's head, and scrubs the youngster. Sure, she must wash thirty or forty kids, most of whom are girls, but what else does she have to do? Once in a while, she gets to take a break from bathing the older kids to comfort the crying infants.

Think about it, those women do not go to the gym or own home trainers, so of course, they can devote more time to cooking. And washing clothes by hand, including dirty diapers, is excellent exercise. Plus, there are no tables, chairs, or sofas to wipe or vacuum. The children eat, play, and learn on the floor, but they sleep in beds, and yes, those must be made.

Apart from the innovative bathing procedure, the women have developed an admirable method for feeding babies who can sit up on their own. First, they place the children in groups of three on the linoleum. Then they set down a bowl and spoon in front of each child. The tots huddle together and pant expectantly as their caregiver sits down and arranges her sari. The moment she picks up a spoon, shiny eyes eagerly track its trajectory. There's no need to play zoom, zoom airplane. As with baby birds, all mouths open automatically. After the meal, they whisk the children off to potty chairs, and the caregivers get two minutes of downtime before receiving an infant and a bottle of milk.

Naturally, the women must scrub the entire orphanage; however, they do that while the children are napping. Cooking for and feeding dozens of children each day must be relaxing. I know this to be true because the caregivers smiled often and appeared to be happy.

We're in the midst of a food reformation. I think our culinary future is promising—three cheers for food blogs, cooking tutorials, and series featuring famous chefs. At last, I know how to make kale the life of the party. Cooking is no longer a burden; it's a global food adventure. Vegetarianism has graduated from nerdy to mainstream. Michelin is plucking stars from hog heaven and handing them to plant eaters. Even vegans have a star in the food sky. It is no longer necessary to eat creatures that live in misery. Happy meat from humanely raised animals is readily available. Do we wish to be hostages of convenience foods or farmer's market explorers? Lucky for us, we all hold the key to our shackles. Bon appétit!

Sleep

Every night, before going to bed, we toss our cherry pit pillows into the microwave and are rewarded with piping hot bags of stones in less than three minutes. In the spirit of German tradition, we never heat the bedroom, so the sheets are icy cold and uninviting all winter. Shivering, I climb into bed, wedge the hot pillow between my feet and burrow into the down comforter. Once again, my husband opens the window despite January's bitter cold. "We'll sleep better in the fresh air," he says. It's below freezing outside, but that's how it is in Germany, another night, another open window.

After a lifetime of sleeping in overheated rooms, it took some getting used to. Supposedly, sleeping in a cold room slows down the aging process, that is, if you don't die of pneumonia first. I consider myself fortunate because a friend of ours grew up in a Tyrolean farmhouse warmed solely by a wood-burning ceramic stove. At night, he and his siblings slept in an unheated attic bedroom under a leaking roof that let in a tad of snow. No doubt, the air was freezing, but down blankets and wool caps worked like a charm. My ten-year-old self wouldn't have worn a nightcap unless it had matched my sky-blue baby doll pajamas.

There are tremendous discrepancies in the places where I've slept. I can only say that exhaustion does not guarantee a good night's sleep, especially when you're lying on the floor of a moving train. Even so, when I was twenty-five, sleeping on a flat, albeit not entirely hygienic surface, was preferable to sitting up all night. Falling asleep begins with a relaxed state of wakefulness. By the time you reach the deep sleep stage, you have lost your muscle tone and can't hold yourself up very well. Hence, the unappealing flopping of your head onto a stranger's shoulders during a long trip. I'd rather be stepped on than slept on.

Our ancestors risked their lives to sleep recumbent. It all began about two million years ago when a biped with a vision, or a bad back, vacated his treetop digs and sprawled out on the ground. I must say, this was one giant leap for mankind. While we may have been safe from predators in our high-rise crash pads, ground sleep enabled us to spend more time in the REM stage, which led to some of us becoming smarter.

Not only did our terrestrial beds alleviate the fear of falling, but they were infinitely more comfortable. Strangely enough, as soon as we moved out of the trees, we began chopping them down. The world sure would be prettier if we had remained in our lofts.

Upon discovering the joys of ground sleeping, our hominid ancestors, as pragmatic as ever, fashioned beds from natural fibers, such as plants and straw. One day, as was bound to happen, Thor's wife draped a bearskin rug over the mattress, and voilà, prehistoric bedding was born. Thor was thrilled and suggested they celebrate her ingenuity with a roll in the hay. These days, accommodations in treehouse hotels cost a fortune. Being close to nature is pricy, considering there isn't much left.

I'm not finicky, but the thought of spending another night in a tent makes me shudder. When you've reached the end of your prime, bucolic surroundings don't compensate for discomfort. Besides, I've developed an affection for memory foam beds and flush toilets. And with a wide variety of nice hotels to choose from, why would I sleep on a foam mat and rest my head on a rolled-up sweatshirt? Because parents will do almost anything for their offspring. Spending the night amid spectacular scenery is undeniably romantic. Then again, you sleep outside in the weather, and unlike your hotel's heating and cooling units, you can't control it.

One year, we drove across the country to show our kids the American West. After a strenuous day exploring the Grand Canyon, we returned to our campsite and struggled to pitch a tent on rocky terrain. I won't bore you with the details, but this endeavor took infinitely longer than planned.

Seeing as we still had primal needs to satisfy, we piled into the car and drove to the rustic yet thoroughly well-stocked Grand Canyon Market Plaza. Their lavish selection rivaled that of any upscale metropolitan supermarket. In true hunting and gathering style, we rounded up some grass-fed steaks, fingerling potatoes, and peppery arugula, then returned to our campsite to build a fire. As soon as the meat hit the grill, it began to rain. Unwilling to go hungry, we hurriedly put the meal together and ate inside our steamy car. All I can say is try cutting wettish steaks on soggy paper plates balanced precariously on your lap. Public Radio entertained us as puddles merged to form a pond beneath our tent.

By nightfall, our insufferable dwelling was an island. "Would you rather sit in a dry car or stretch out in a wet tent?" I asked my family. "We want a real adventure. Let's sleep in the tent," my son said. Well, what do you know, our polyester chalet was not waterproof. Rain saturated the fabric throughout the night, and water dripped onto our faces. Not only that, howling coyotes disrupted our already fitful sleep. Early the following morning, native birdsong roused us. Hardly, our backwoods alarm clock played the sound of slamming RV doors. There is nothing peaceful about camping with hundreds of people: we packed our sodden belongings and fled.

Although I have a lot on my mind when trying to fall asleep, one thing I don't have to worry about is being eaten. Horses get their shuteye standing up in case they need to run like hell. Cows, on the other hand, have only us to fear. Therefore, our bovine friends can lounge on the grass all night because ignorance really is bliss. I have no idea how flamingoes get any sleep standing on one skinny leg. Supposedly, their joints snap into place, and gravity keeps them upright. Gravity has the opposite effect on me, especially when I'm tired. In fact, I can barely balance on one leg while applying lotion to the bottom of my foot. Still, nothing beats sea otters for cuteness; those cherubic creatures sleep holding hands.

I am not a prolific sleeper. Whiling away sixteen hours in bed, like an armadillo or a teenager, would exhaust rather than rejuvenate me. I haven't slept that much since I was in utero. Odds are, my embryonic self was already hyper. Only a handful of people possess genes that enable them to survive on the bare minimum, which appears to be six hours or fewer. According to sleep scientists, we need between seven and eight hours of sleep a night. Tell this to my internal chronometer.

I'd like to add that I'm a glutton for silence when it comes to sleeping, and wearing headphones to bed is unthinkable. On the flip side, my kids need music thumping in their ears in order to relax. My daughter even cleans her room with one hand and carries her phone in the other because the task is too daunting without a motivating beat.

We live in a village, and other than the occasional barking dog or drunken reveler stumbling home from the train station, it is relatively peaceful. Although, I never considered a quiet neighborhood a liability until we had an overnight guest from Los Angeles. Our California friend could not fall asleep until my husband began practicing the violin in the morning. "I need the sound of sirens and helicopters to help me sleep," he said matter-of-factly. "Fortunately, the violin worked just as well."

Falling asleep has become more difficult with age, even when lying on a fabulous mattress in a quiet room, cradling a hot cherry pit pillow. Ultimately, I wish I could sleep like our dog, anywhere, anytime, and on the spot.

Cutlery and Friends

T able etiquette is not an inborn trait. Toddlers pleasurably squeeze food between their tiny fingers, then toss it onto the floor. They lick their plates, slurp water from the dog's bowl, and fling oatmeal around the kitchen. Eating is uninhibited and carefree.

Go ahead, Buttercup, bang your fork, and enjoy your culinary fireworks because your last rambunctious supper is around the corner. It's time you learned some table manners.

Growing up, I was unaware that a variety of dining styles existed. Like everyone we knew, my family ate American style, which, in retrospect, entailed quite an elaborate cutlery routine. This is how it works; lift the fork with your left hand, turn a little pirouette so the tines face downward, then spear my mother's thoroughly cooked roast. (Food was well done in her quest to obliterate trichinosis and salmonella.) Next, use the knife-wielding right hand to saw the meat. I'll wait a moment for you to accomplish this task because it's tough. Now relegate the knife to the plate's edge, transfer the fork to your right hand and turn up the tines. If you happen to be in the mood for a very soft green bean, poke it now. Al dente was not a thing in the sixties, at least not in the Midwest. Nevertheless, my mother's kitchen floor was paved with good intentions and Clorox.

If you want to bypass the swapping routine, simply use the fork's edge to cut soft edibles. On second thought, that might not be proper dining etiquette. I'm also not sure whether coaxing stray peas onto the fork with your index finger is a no-go. Then again, peas are little balls, and unless they are nudged onto the fork, they will roll wildly around your plate. I suggest you wait until nobody is looking, then stab those little pod dwellers. Despite my uncertainty about dining customs, I know this: purgatory awaits those who lick their plates. Thou shalt not slurp, burp, or chomp at the table. Mouths are not blowholes; the food will cool down if you give it a minute. And I urge you to seal your lips when chewing. In the end, nothing beats gnawing meat off a bone alone in the kitchen.

Following my wedding, I moved to Europe, and in order to assimilate, I had to modify my table protocol. It's not as if I wiped my face with the tablecloth, but I did not eat in the continental style, meaning, fork in the left hand, knife in the right, and both utensils engaged at all times. My husband encouraged me to try.

"Admittedly, the symmetry of the continental approach beats our labor-intensive switching. Still, dining that way feels awkward and takes the fun out of eating."

"You can do it," my husband said. "Finding your mouth with your left hand can't be that difficult."

"Well, it is. Why can't we eat like Americans?"

"Because we live in Europe."

"I have learned to drive a stick shift. Does it matter how I eat a bratwurst?"

"I suppose not," he replied dejectedly.

Then it dawned on me, "What about a creative hybrid?"

"How might that look?"

"I'd hold the fork in my right hand and the knife in my left. No more swapping. And, of course, I'd spear fries with the fork and rest my wrists on the edge of the table, clearly displaying the absence of a weapon. Then, before the first bite, I'd proclaim guten appetit."

"Okay, let's see how it goes."

Certain culinary situations remained significantly stressful, like the time I was invited to dine at a Michelin-starred restaurant with out-of-town relatives I had never met. I indulged in mouthwatering food fantasies until I realized that Tantris was not the kind of place suited to my hybrid eating style. No one would openly judge me. Nevertheless, they would scrutinize my behavior, and I dreaded the evening. My grandparents were Polish, Lithuanian, British, and German and readily adapted to everything American, including dining etiquette. In the spirit of my forefathers, I was determined to prove my versatility. During the subway ride to the restaurant, I screwed up the courage to eat like a European. This was a grave mistake. Not only was I incapable of walking elegantly in high heels after a lifetime of wearing flats, but switching cutlery hands without prior practice was foolish. I set out to do both in a figure-hugging, itchy wool pencil skirt, blazer, and nylon stockings, all of which I loathe.

The waiter placed the menu in my trembling hands, and I scanned it for the most uncomplicated fare to eat in public. The baked songbird was out of the question. It wasn't that a singing bird was less palatable than a clucking chicken, but I was unsure how to eat it. Consuming an entire animal can be a challenge. Lobster is the first thing that comes to mind. What if the songbird came with extra tools for breaking its tiny bones? I couldn't risk it.

Thus, I remained in my comfort zone and selected a meat and potatoes dish. I did not regret my decision, for the humble spud was transformed into a cloud of potatoes topped with a crunchy potato hat. Proudly, I held the fork in my left hand, scooped up a little mound of fluff, and ever so leisurely, maneuvered it into my mouth. It was utterly delicious. My languid eating manner could be interpreted as elegance rather than caution. The meat, unfortunately, posed a dilemma because it had to be cut. Over the years, I had become accustomed to cutting with my left hand and abruptly felt confused. I watched my fellow diners and tried to imitate them without calling attention to myself. I'm an imposter; I wanted to shout, but I couldn't recall the word in German.

Navigating the meal in three languages and speaking only two amplified my misery. It was like putting on makeup while riding a skateboard.

When the dessert menu arrived, I ordered a confection that I considered safe. The waiter brought a plate of creamy decadence decorated with an upside-down cone. Now what? Do I pick up the cone with my fingers or use silverware? Weren't cones invented to forgo silverware? How does one grasp a cone with cutlery? "What's the matter with you?" my inner voice scolded. "Pick it up already." And so I did, a little too roughly. The chilly pink filling oozed onto my thumb and index finger, yet everyone acted like nothing had happened.

You know, the next time I'm invited to dinner, I'll suggest an Indian restaurant. I wonder whether I should eat with my left or right hand?

Cold Sheep Days

In Bavaria, people believe there is no such thing as miserable weather, only inadequate clothing. Wintertime brings babies wrapped in sheepskin bunting bags, gurgling cheerfully in strollers while their parents sip hot spiced wine at frosty outdoor markets. "Finally, a real winter," Fritz says lightheartedly as snowflakes dust his greasy bratwurst. Bavarians pretty much dislike winters that are too balmy. They dream of frozen ponds, snowy slopes, and dreadful woolen undergarments. I'd rather eat a slug than torment my body with a wool undershirt. Even watching my husband slip that scratchy thing over his head is insufferable. In my hometown, a suburb of Cleveland, inclement weather was met with grumpiness and polyester.

One frigid January evening, I received a call from an excited neighbor, "Lake Deixlfurt is frozen. Grab your skates and meet us there in twenty minutes. I'm bringing a thermos of grog."

I was more afraid than opposed.

"For one thing, Ina, that's a big lake, and for another, it's pitch-black outside. We won't see cracks in the ice."

"Don't worry, there's a full moon tonight."

"The air is bitterly cold. Why don't we drink your thermos of grog in my overheated kitchen instead?"

"We'll have a great time," she said before hanging up.

Sure, it sounded romantic, but that's precisely what passengers felt when boarding the Titanic. The promise of adventure overrode fear because our offspring were ready and waiting at the door in record-breaking time. We piled into the car wearing puffy down jackets and drove to the lake.

I must admit, the moonlit lake was stunning, but it groaned and emitted explosive cracks that reverberated across the frozen void. The pond where we usually skated never sounded like this. We stood on the shore like a herd of spindly-legged sheep, uncertain whether sliding around on a rumbling body of water was a good idea, especially at night.

Our friends arrived, and we squeezed into our skates. No one broached the subject of safety. Finally, I said, "The lake is making creepy noises. It doesn't sound safe."

Ina was unconcerned. "The ice is shifting, that's all." Then, she darted onto the deathtrap, followed by my husband and kids. Warily, I shuffled onto the black ice. Whirling around in the moonlight was like a scene from a Disney film, but the thunderstorm underfoot was impossible to ignore. You can't choose how you will die. At the same time, you can avoid death on a frozen lake by getting off it. And that's exactly what I did. Then I shed my skates and helped myself to some grog.

The weather never hinders my son's activities; it governs them. On absurdly cold winter mornings, he lugs his skis to the train station where he meets his friends for a two-hour trip to the mountains. Upon reaching the slopes, they slap strips of synthetic fur onto their skis and trudge up the hill. According to them, chairlifts are boring. The trek takes around six hours and is fueled by half-frozen sandwiches. Ski mountaineering is the name of the sport.

The night before the outing, I go into his bedroom to say goodnight and notice a thin fleece shirt and ski pants draped over the chair.

"Is that what you're wearing?"

"Yeah, that's it."

"You'll get pneumonia traipsing up that hill without a coat," I whine.

"Actually, we work up a sweat. Besides, I have a jacket in my backpack for the descent."

"Those backcountry trails are prone to avalanches. Why can't you take the lift like everyone else?"

"We have shovels to dig each other out in case anything happens. Anyway, avalanches aren't predicted."

"Accidents are not predictable; otherwise, they wouldn't happen."

"Yeah, but doing stuff that's too easy isn't fun either."

Despite my best efforts, I have never overcome my fear of the mountains. I wish the Alps were inanimate rocks, but they are moody beauties. On top of inherent undulations, their inner cores are melting. Ice is the glue that holds their cracks, crevices, and remotest parts together, and it is liquefying. The last time I went hiking, the snow looked like it was blushing, so I removed my rose-colored glasses. Lo-and-behold, the mountain was covered in pink algae, yet another symptom of an ailing planet.

Summer is when our progeny takes to the hills on his bike. One year, he and his fellow physicists cycled from Munich to Barcelona. Over the next thousand miles, they crossed the Alps and the Pyrenees while enduring narrow winding roads, scorching sun, and drizzling rain. At the end of the day, nothing beats camping in the wilderness. (Ironically, the one time they stayed at an official campsite, most of their gear was stolen.) Clearly, the forest is the world's most picturesque toilet. And who needs a shower when you have a bathtub the size of a river, let alone one that is a river. Everyone knows there's nothing better than spaghetti cooked on a camp stove infused with the scent of funky cycling apparel. Finally, allow me to introduce you to the pinnacle of rustic outdoor slumber: the pop-up tent. That baby transforms into lodgings with a mere flick of the wrist.

Growing up in Ohio, sledding was about as adventurous as it got. We never wore knitwear made of scratchy wool or burrowed into billowy down blankets like our ancestors from the old country; we turned up the thermostat. The furnace blew hot air through ducts in the wall and dried out our eyeballs as we sat on the dining room floor in front of the vent, chatting on the phone about the dismal weather.

Summer's oppressive heat was conquered with a whirling dervish of ceiling and oscillating fans. I remember my father mounting a large fan in the attic window, convinced that it would draw the hot air out of the room, and cool down the entire house. Since we weren't sweating less, it may have had a placebo effect. Years after I moved out, my parents installed whole-house air conditioning, but I missed the fans and open windows when I returned to visit. Hermetically sealed houses make me feel like I'm trapped inside a Tupperware container.

Most German buildings lack air conditioning, and our house is no exception. We have dog days, but I use a small, portable misting fan for those. You fill its tiny tank with water and bask in the cooling vapor it blows in your face, and only your face, unless you are the size of a Barbie doll.

Ode to May in Ohio. Lilacs and mild temperatures pull us out of our winter torpor. We wear shorts and repulse each other with unsightly, and in some cases, unshaven pale legs. Rust is scraped from the grill, and patio furniture is doused with bleach, my mother's best-loved cleaner. Still, the effort is worth it. All summer, we enjoy the view from the air-conditioned dining room.

In my neck of the woods, May flirts with both summer and winter. So, when a Bavarian wakes up in the middle of the month to frigid temperatures and slate gray skies, he shrugs and blames the Ice Saints.

"Today is the cold Sophie. What did you expect?"

"We had the same weather yesterday, didn't we?"

"Well, that was the cold Bonifatius."

"And what about tomorrow?"

"Are you going to let the cold Servatius get you down?"

Not to be outdone, June teases us with beach weather. Then, around the middle of the month, polar air sweeps down from the north, and summer comes to a grinding halt. I'm fed up, but Bavarians nonchalantly don a wool sweater and announce the arrival of the *Schafskälte*, or *Cold Sheep Days*. Year after frigid year, when mid-June rolls around, farmers shear their sheep. This cold snap has been occurring with eighty-nine percent accuracy for centuries, yet sheep owners continue to strip the poor animals of their fleece. What's the rush? Knitting season doesn't begin until September, and it's not as if we have a yarn shortage.

Sheep are generous providers. For starters, their two tiny teats produce the milk we need to make feta and pecorino cheese. The slightly piquant Spanish Manchego is a feat of sheer magic. Mary's little lamb perishes for our Easter lunch and is subjected to the degradation of being dipped in mint sauce. A staggering quantity of lamb kibble feeds our hungry pets. Do pet food manufacturers really mix lamb, which costs an arm and a leg, with soybeans, cereals, and grains to make dry dog food? I'd be willing to bet that mutton is the main ingredient in Fifi's victuals.

Sheep have been keeping us warm and fashionable for thousands of years. After being domesticated, they lost their ability to shed and rely on us for haircuts. You'd think we could be more accommodating and not make them run around naked during a polar windstorm.

Come summer, Bavarians flock to beer gardens to sip Pilsner and nibble on king-sized pretzels. When the mercury dips to sobering levels, heating columns and woolly blankets, probably infested with mites, make it all very cozy. Allow me to reiterate; there is no such thing as dreadful weather, just inferior clothing. Once, when hiking with my husband's family, I complained about walking in the rain. Water was running in rivulets down my nylon pants and into my shoes. It was my mother-in-law who reminded me I was not made of sugar and, therefore, would not melt.

I hasten to add that Bavarians get cranky when it rains day after lousy day. They call it dauerregen, which means forever rain. Flat nimbostratus clouds, the color of tarnished lead, obscure the sun, resulting in ongoing precipitation and darkness, which in turn causes likable people to behave like donkeys.

Lately, Bavaria is getting soaked while the rest of the country is drying up. Earth almighty is more fragile than we imagined, though our sheep are remarkably resilient.

There's something appealing about sheep. They are not dim-witted and always have a positive attitude. Even when we shear them on a cold day, they answer with a profound Baaaaa.

Folly

Nearly forty years ago, I jumped into an abandoned limestone quarry filled with cloudy, turquoise-hued water. I was eighteen and just beginning my studies at Indiana University in Bloomington. Numerous retired limestone pits encircle the town and lure students despite repeated injuries and fatalities. They are unlike anything I have ever seen. Visibility below the surface is less than two inches, and the frigid water takes your breath away. So, how can you wave your arms hysterically and scream like a banshee when you're hypothermic? You can't. That's why you drown unnoticed until you're spotted floating on the surface by an intoxicated freshman who thinks you're a Hoosier with an incomparable ability to hold your breath.

The Empire State Building, Yankee Stadium, and dozens more iconic American structures were constructed using Indiana limestone. Would you leap into an opaque pool the depth of Yankee Stadium? Swimming in the quarries was strictly forbidden, and ubiquitous no trespassing signs couldn't be missed. Regardless, thrill seekers and grandstanders plunged sixty-five feet to their deaths, diving from the legendary rooftop cliff every summer. Built-in pools also have sheer walls, but your excavator didn't remove eighteen thousand tons of stone for your little rectangle, then fill it with murky water and debris.

Nevertheless, I found myself pedaling through Indiana's back roads on a battered bike alongside a dental student who convinced me that quarry swimming would change my life. Only if it doesn't end it, I thought.

When we neared the pit, we leaned our bikes against a tree and ran. It was a wild place, and the explosion of beauty got your heart racing. Sheer walls of granite, teal blue water, and foliage bulging from rock crevasses mingled with harebrained college students to create a bucolic wonderland. Pine and deciduous trees shared the periphery, and the intoxicating scent of conifers and cannabis added to the euphoria. The quarry was definitely a showstopper.

"The water is stunning, but I can't see beneath the surface," I said nervously.

"Don't worry, I know where the rocks are."

"Those are not rocks, they're boulders, the size of refrigerators. Look how they're jutting out of the water at weird angles."

He grinned, "Trust me, it's safe where we're jumping in."

"When it's hot, the water level drops and the slabs are closer to the surface. Have you considered that?"

"I've done this before. We'll be fine."

"Surely animals fall in. Do you want to swim in water contaminated by decomposing bodies? Why don't we just sit here and admire the view?"

"Come on, let's go."

I didn't want to risk my life for this experience, yet I did. We stood up, flung off our clothes, and headed for the cliff's edge.

"I feel like a cat about to regurgitate a hairball."

"Jump," he cried.

Warily, I leaped into the spine-chilling water. A jackhammer pounded in my chest, and the turbid liquid engulfed my limbs. My barely submerged hands were invisible. After a few strokes, I panicked.

"I have to get out," I yelped.

He pointed at some rocks and said, "You can climb out over there," and then he swam away.

I hoisted myself onto a stone ledge protruding from the blueberry slushie and clambered out.

What motivated me to do this? Adventures are the status symbols of youth. But my main concern was missing out on something. Aside from that, public displays of fear, better known as peer pressure, are humiliating when you're young.

Several years later, I was a finalist in a writing competition, and the sponsors flew me to an event in Hawaii. I jogged on pristine beaches, hiked through secluded bamboo forests, and collected lava rocks. Traveling, coupled with the exotic scenery, enticed me to let my hair down. In other words, I threw caution to the island's trade winds. While strolling along the beach, I noticed a group of college kids standing in a circle. I nudged my way into the pack and was amazed to see a crater about six feet deep and just as wide. The hole accommodated three people.

"What is this?" I asked no one in particular.

"It's a blowhole. When waves break along the shore, they send water rushing into the lava tubes that run like plumbing underneath the island. The tube feeding this hole creates some serious magic; watch what happens next," the ringleader said with a grin.

A geyser launched three giggling girls into the air, then scattered them on the sand. The instigator suggested I give it a shot.

"This is not a good idea," my rational inner voice whispered.

Without a second thought, I hopped into the hole and waited. Water rushed through the tubes, hurtled me into the air, and tossed me onto the beach.

"That was amazing."

"You know, sometimes it's not the right type of wave, and people don't get propelled out of the hole, they get sucked underground into a lava tube," the boy beside me muttered.

"Do they get trapped underneath the island?"

"Yeah, sometimes they do," he said without turning to look at me.

Walking along the coast, I chastised myself for assuming the stunt was safe. But my exploit was quickly forgotten. The ocean looked magnificent, and I darted into the surf, dove through a wave, and swam with abandon.

After a while, I saw a sign perched on a rock—*Only Strong Swimmers Beyond This Point*. I'm a decent swimmer, I thought, and continued to breaststroke my way through increasingly choppy water. Breathing became difficult as waves forced water up my nose, so I decided to return to the beach. When I turned around, it shocked me to see how far away the shore appeared to be.

"Sure is jackass. Remember when you failed the lifeguard test and ended up waitressing all summer precisely because you lacked strength," my sensible turned smart-alecky voice jeered.

"Pipe down. I don't need to be castigated by you. Where were you a half-hour ago?"

My efforts against the current were in vain. Growing up, I swam in Lake Erie, and sure, there were undertows, but now I was fighting waves governed by the moon. I changed my stroke to the crawl and thrashed through the swells. Ironically, I was thrust into the slab bearing the strong swimmer sign. Surges hurled me repeatedly into the boulder, and the barnacles protruding from the rock scraped my legs. I looked around and discovered that I was alone. As far as the eye could see, no boats, surfers, or swimmers were in the water.

Having reached the shore, I sat on the sand, panting. I attribute the fact that I didn't drown to sheer luck and not survival of the fittest.

The pesky voice of reason couldn't resist a final jab. "You mingled rather casually among the sharks. I'm impressed."

"You're so melodramatic."

"Ha! Hardly. Take a look at your legs. They're bleeding. You were on the lunch menu, sweetheart."

Excuses

A friend called to invite me to her skincare party, but I wasn't home, so she left a message on my answering machine. Themed parties are more tedious than knitting and instigate my flight response. The problem is, I tend to accept invitations, even when I prefer to pass. Not this time. I returned my friend's call, "Sorry, I can't make it to your party because I'm attending a violin recital." There is no need to sugarcoat that reply. Reasons are powerful, unbending, and solitary. It took me decades to figure that out, and after I did, I felt like a draft horse freed from its cart.

My entire life, I have been accommodating people for fear of hurting their feelings. Once in a while, I've stumbled out of an unwanted engagement. "Hopelessly busy, blah, blah, blah, very stressed, coming down with the flu. Maybe we can meet for coffee sometime." Wasn't that an impressive display of gumption? When I cannot summon the courage to say no and attend a maddening event, regret, and resentment inevitably put me in a terrible mood. After sniveling to a friend about my self-inflicted burdens, she said, "You don't have to drink curdled milk if you don't want to. Just stop it."

"Besides drinking sour milk, I usually ask for more and reciprocate for the sake of decorum," I squeaked.

Freedom from the inability to say no has always been a fantasy of mine. Whenever I lacked a bona fide reason for declining an invitation, I always accepted. That's no longer the case. My days of concocting clumsy excuses are over. Another thing is that I no longer let manipulative people exhaust me into submission by chopping away at my perfectly valid reason. "Oh c'mon, my party will be awesome. Would you mind leaving your event a little early?"

"Sorry, I can't."

It's incredible how easy this is and how guilt-free I feel. Age is empowering. Although, age wasn't the only factor that stopped me from placating others. Neither was it resignation, indifference, or a lack of stamina. Instead, my new lifestyle was shaped by an epiphany. One day, I woke up and saw the glaring light of mortality twinkling at the end of the proverbial tunnel. "You are sixty years old, and life is no longer infinite," said the Grim Reaper. "Start driving the car. It's your road trip." And then the angel of death morphed into the hood ornament.

Certain obligations are unavoidable, but if ironing shirts sounds more appealing, don't cave in. A bouquet of excuses is unnecessary. Did your phone just ring, ding, or ping? Sit tight. You are not Pavlov's dog, resist the urge to answer. Your friend will leave a message, and you'll have plenty of time to mull over their request. We're vulnerable when caught off guard. Of course, we don't want to lie. We only wish to protect ourselves. So, fix yourself a cup of hemp tea and devise a tender reason for not attending the Proust reading your friend's son is giving at the local library. Should the happy herb make you brave, you can always be candid and say, "I can't go because I don't feel like it." I'm about as likely to utter that sentence as I am to share an ice cream cone with a pet.

I should also mention that the excuses I tell myself are unrivaled. My convoluted brain is perpetually thwarting my self-control and sabotaging my willpower. Isn't that organ supposed to be looking out for my well-being? For example, a local chocolatier bathes caramelized hazelnuts in a tub of creamy Swiss milk chocolate and then molds the delicious goo into slabs the size of placemats. My husband occasionally brings one home, and as soon as that confection enters our house, it has me firmly in its grip. I break off a sizable chunk and gobble it up like a dog gulping down a purloined meat-loaf. Why? Because I had a tough week, and I have the right to indulge myself once in a while, and because I'm a damned genius at justifying lust. I'm guessing that self-destruction begins with rationalization and a flood of happy hormones. I have a big brain theory; my frolicking gray matter could care less about my burgeoning buttocks and impending diabetes.

In the world of excuses, distraction is also a charming col-laborator. I launch myself into a flurry of activity to avoid the trials and tribulations of a despised task. Suddenly, the dish-washer needs unloading, leaves require raking, and closets beg cleaning. If I were a social media enthusiast, I might escape to cyberspace. Diversion is married to procrastination, and they are a ruthless team. Diversion lures you out of reality, and procrastination hands you a cup of coffee, a piece of cake, and a footstool.

Eventually, I said to myself, enough is enough. From now on, you will not dodge jobs you despise; you will do them first. The following morning, after breakfast, I was tackling some tedious paperwork when the phone rang. Did I wait for the caller to leave a message on my machine? Absolutely not. I answered the phone and let the friend distract me. After a lengthy conversation and several cups of coffee, I had to use the bathroom. Since it was impossible to ignore the mound of dirty clothes bulging from my overflowing laundry basket, I had no choice but to load the washing machine.

When deceiving myself, my excuses are as prolific as Shake-speare's use of iambic pentameter. From now on, I'm follow-ing the advice of our first president; "It's better to offer no ex-cuse than a bad one," George Washington wrote to his niece. Big hug, George. And before we wrap this up, Mr. President, I would like to thank you for your equally irresistible remark: "It's better to be alone than in bad company."

Tricked by Age

When I was young, I whizzed through life on a winged horse without a helmet or a seatbelt. Looking back, I cringe at some of the things I did, such as threading hooks through the bodies of slippery nightcrawlers and lively minnows. Anxious to reel in a perch the size of a marlin, my grandfather and I cast the poor, impaled creatures into the water to be eaten alive. Baitfish and worms were nonentities on par with dough balls. Nowadays, when gardening with a spade, I'm paranoid about slicing through those already legless animals. Children are not enslaved by guilt; it's too disabling. The burden of regret comes later.

There are times when the staticky film reel of my childhood flickers in a dusty niche of my mind and dislodges a remarkably vibrant memory. Cut to Saturday morning. My father is driving our faux-wood paneled station wagon to Cleveland's doughnut wizard, Jack Frost. As far as I'm concerned, Jack's is an artisan bakery minus the trendy interior and a name like La Jacques. Sitting cross-legged on our living room floor while watching *Bugs Bunny* on a television sporting rabbit ears, I couldn't help but think about the euphoria inducing maple cream I was about to devour. A cloud of a doughnut, fried to perfection, glazed with maple icing and topped with whipped cream. Each of us craved, no, downright lusted after that beauty, yet my dad invariably bought an assorted dozen. Those who claim that only children never learn to share did not grow up in a large family where fair distribution took priority.

We lunged at the box as soon as it entered the house, and when four siblings are members of your pack, sharing is not caring, it's aggravating. As for sweets, we could split a pastry more accurately than Einstein an atom. I remember thinking, someday, I will buy an entire box of maple creams and eat them all. Here's the kicker, even though I could afford to fill my kitchen with doughnuts, I prefer to stuff myself with raw salmon instead. Sometimes, it really is too late.

Without a doubt, my amusement park days are over. The wooden coaster of my childhood clocked forty miles per hour and got my heart racing. These days, I'd need a sedative to ride the g-force behemoths that hurl you to the edge of blacking out and make you sick as a dog. My son has the hots for a monstrosity that launches fearless riders to the clouds and then blasts them down a steel mountain at one hundred and twenty miles per hour. It's called the Dragster and should come equipped with a black box. Let's just say if I want my insides turned to salsa, I'll drink from the park's water fountain.

Back when I traveled by bike, summer mornings were muggy with excitement. When school let out in June, my mother put us out to pasture in our cozy suburban neighborhood, which was presumably, but unlikely, free of pedophiles. After breakfast, we ran wild. Since we were too grubby to go inside for lunch, we ate peanut butter and jelly sandwiches at the picnic table and washed them down with a sugary beverage prepared from a package of purple powder.

Scars branded our days, and fear never hampered our freedom. One morning, my brother Jeff, two years my junior, was climbing a chain-link fence and gored his face on a barb jutting from the top rail. Now that I think about it, I have no idea how I freed him from his skewer and carried him home. After being stitched up, he was outside the next day.

Years later, my youngest brother Kevin injured himself popping wheelies on a homemade bike ramp. I was babysitting, and my parents were unreachable since their sole high-tech device was my father's digital wristwatch, which boasted a calculator and not a phone. When Kevin's face turned the color of cream cheese, I wondered whether his injury merited an ambulance. He wasn't bleeding, so I comforted him with cookies until my parents returned and whisked him to the hospital. It turns out that he had broken his arm. For some reason, my nail-biting anxiety regarding injuries began only after I had my own children.

Do I remember all the Christmases of my life? Certainly not, but I do remember the year Santa brought me a glass cutter. I was around ten and spent that holiday vacation decapitating jars and transforming them into drinking glasses cherished only by me. When the novelty wore off, I plugged in my toy oven and pumped out tiny cakes using the heat of a hundred-watt light bulb. Modern light-emitting diodes have rendered that toy obsolete. And then there was Barbie. For hours, I dressed and disrobed that woman, and never once did it cross my mind that future naked me might not look quite as hot.

When does the winding lane of childhood get replaced by the straight and narrow road of destination? Lately, I have less fun but more purpose, and the earnestness of it all is somewhat deflating. Instead of working in the yard, I could sit on the stoop, prod a few pill bugs, and watch them curl into balls. Did you know that these mini crustaceans have gills, are related to shrimp, and sop up the remaining nourishment in their feces. Those overachievers also suck heavy metals from the soil. At one time, prodding pill bugs was a Zen moment. Now, I carry a supercomputer in my pocket, and my need to know must be satiated. By the way, roly-polies are isopods and not insects. "Google isopod, Mommy."

One year, I visited the bungalow where I spent my first decade of life. In no way did this paltry house and square of grass live up to my vivid memory of a sprawling lawn and spacious home. The disparity between memory and reality is not subtle. Again, I've been tricked by age.

Speaking of being tricked, fifty years ago, I chewed five hundred wads of bubble gum and diligently saved the wrappers for a free real camera. We may grow forgetful, whereas childhood injustices park themselves in the hippocampus for eternity. I remember sitting on the lawn counting those waxy little papers, stuffing them into an envelope, and mailing them to the Bubblehead Corporation. Every damned day, I waited for the arrival of that camera. Even after a year had passed, I naively looked forward to the day I would come home from school to my Bubblehead package. Then it became clear to me that the Bubblehead people were evil villains who disenchanted children by making them chew gum until their teeth rotted, then left them despondent and distrustful of promotional giveaways for the rest of their lives. Maybe the post office lost my wrappers. Perhaps the package was delivered to the wrong address, and an undeserving child without cavities started a career as a Pulitzer prize-winning photographer with my *free real camera*.

Childhood is not all giggles and ice cream, but it's certainly the last time people will call your potbelly cute. Now, that's something to chew on.

Odd Jobs

When I was a teenager, I was seduced by the notion of working at McDonald's. In my sixteen-year-old mind, making french fries in smoldering grease would be far more rewarding than babysitting. Before you could say cheeseburger, I submitted an application for employment and was elated to be hired immediately after the interview.

A week later, a crew trainer ushered me to the back room, where I joined a brood of fledgling burger builders to learn the tricks of the trade. Following my enlightenment, he gave me a job at the front counter. I remember taking orders and tallying them on a pad of paper. I recall the snaking line of hungry people didn't bring out the best in my abysmal math skills. And I know for a fact that many of my customers never paid the correct amount for their food. Exasperated parents struggling with screaming offspring and a tottering tray of drinks didn't care about receiving the proper change. In all fairness, how was I supposed to excel at arithmetic in a madhouse when I couldn't do better than a C on a math test taken in a quiet classroom? Why the man put me up front before evaluating my skills, say with a stack of flashcards, remains an enigma.

Aside from the job magnifying my shortcomings, my friends were earning more money waitressing. After six weeks, and without a trace of regret, I stopped working for the world's largest fast-food chain to become a waitress at Friendly's. This position came with a blue and white checkered dress and a ruffled apron that made me look like a chambermaid. I couldn't wait to reap the fiscal advantages of waitressing.

Friendly's served burgers and bland meals similar to cafeteria fare. My first customer was an elderly man burdened by his own existence. I handed him the menu, set down a complimentary glass of water, and returned a few minutes later to take his order. He barked his request, and I submitted the order to the kitchen staff. They immediately informed me of my first infraction. "You forgot to ask him whether he wants fries or mashed potatoes."

I returned to the man's table to inquire about his preference. He was not amused.

"Mashed," he growled.

"Mashed," I told the cooks. Next, they asked, "What kind of salad dressing does he want?"

"You've got to be kidding me. That means I'll have to disturb that ornery man again."

I walked back to his table and said, "I'm sorry for bothering you. It's my first day. What kind of salad dressing would you like?"

He waved me away like a housefly and spat, "Ranch."

After he finished his meal, I asked, "Could I interest you in dessert or coffee?"

He shook an arthritic finger at me and said, "You are the worst waitress I have ever had." Then, he slammed a penny on the table.

I am proud to say that I did not cry in front of him. But, in terms of life lessons, this one was jarring: Never forget the spud when your customer is a mean old dud.

Friendly restaurants feature fishbowls of ice cream doused in several sauces and topped with whipped cream. Sometimes, women asked me whether the strawberry sauce had fewer calories than the chocolate. "Yes, it sure does," I would say with authority because I learned early on to tell them what they wanted to hear.

Occasionally, the wrong sauce or flavor of ice cream landed in the bowl, and an irate customer sent it back. I smiled and said, "My apologies. The kitchen staff made this mistake, and they will correct it." Why shouldn't I blame the kitchen? They weren't on the front lines and never had to endure customer backlash. As a bonus, the mistake provided a snack for all the waitresses, and we wolfed it down with relish. Forty years later, I writhe at the thought of the bacterial soup in that bowl.

After a few weeks, I learned to predict my customers' behavior. Guys on dates were polite and left excellent tips. Old
women often plunked a quarter beside their plates, regardless of the meal's price or quality of service. Daddies grinned
sheepishly before tossing a crumpled dollar bill on the sticky
table. Go, Daddy, go away, and don't come back. After I had
my wisdom teeth pulled, I had a black and blue face that
not only made hungry patrons uncomfortable but also made
them splendid tippers.

My shift usually ended at midnight. When I got home,
I'd empty my pockets onto the bedroom floor. It felt like
winning the lottery. Before going to bed, I tallied my wealth
and took pleasure in uncrumpling the bills and building tidy
towers of coins. My body was exhausted, but my brain was in
overdrive. Throughout the night, I vacillated between wakefulness and sleep. There were times when I saw my server
number illuminated above my bedroom door. Burgers were
getting cold, ice cream was melting, and I was trapped in bed
with orders tumbling around my head.

Nearly every weekend for two years, I served meals to my
fellow man, woman, and child and suffered their whims.
Finally, upon graduating from high school, I bid Friendly's
farewell.

A month later, I went to college and segued directly into
a food service job in my dorm's kitchen, a position which
entailed plucking sizable cockroaches from the cottage cheese
before plopping the stainless steel module into the buffet
trough. "By the way, that's not pepper on top of the curds, it's

turds. Not only are you eating cockroach feces, but I'm not ashamed to say that we have no qualms about serving food that has fallen onto the floor," I warned my unsuspecting friends.

A string of monotonous jobs followed. My stint as a stagehand lasted a week. When the boss realized I couldn't lift the massive sets, he suggested I repair torn stage curtains instead. "I've sewn doll clothes and embroidered napkins, so yeah, I can do that." He led me through the dimly lit corridors to a dingy backstage room where an industrial sewing machine and a heap of dusty drapes were parked in a corner. "Those curtains need mending. The machine is easy to use. You'll figure it out." He turned and left without saying another word.

I was determined to be a competent drape mender, but when I tried lifting the top curtain, it wouldn't budge. Grand drapes are made of velvet, they're the size of a tennis court, and their weight is staggering. My biceps have the circumference of a banana. Why did the manager hire a scrawny girl to work as a stagehand, I wondered.

I may not have strength, but I do have perseverance. I grabbed a corner of the curtain and pulled it across the floor looking for tears in the fabric. As soon as I discovered a gash, I'd heave the cloth onto the platform of the sewing machine, an instrument of self-mutilation in the wrong hands, and try to stitch it without puckering the fabric. Puffs of dust wafted into my face, turning my nasal membranes black. I quit to avoid the humiliation of being fired.

My roommate was a guard at a local art museum and told me they were looking for a person to oversee the top floor galleries.

"What exactly am I supposed to do?"

"Stroll around and make sure no one touches the paintings."

"How much does it pay?"

"Four bucks an hour. No uniform, just look good."

"Then how do the visitors recognize me as the voice of authority?"

"Your name tag says guard."

Before long, I was on my way to the museum armed with comfortable shoes and the words, don't touch. Since the place was never packed, I could easily monitor my flock of art grazers. The best part of the job was eavesdropping on poignant and insightful assessments of paintings, dull sermons about art, and self-aggrandizing connoisseurs wishing to show off their expertise. I savored the museum's silence and enjoyed an intimate relationship with a few paintings, but the hands of the clock moved more slowly than an oyster. Wait a minute, oysters don't move. It lasted six months.

My low-brow jobs were about as much fun as getting a colonoscopy. First, let me say that I'm sorry to have sold my blood. I did contribute to developments in psychology by participating in experiments for the psych department. Human guinea pigs received ten dollars for their services. In addition, I played the clarinet in park bands, taught clarinet, completed a master's in clarinet, and freelanced in orchestras. Still, my income as a musician had to be supplemented.

Although I dislike talking on the phone, I applied for a job doing exactly that. My alma mater hired me to contact alumni and solicit donations for the fine institution that enlightened them. At some point, I traded that phone job for another and began working for a quirky piano tuner who carried Bach's *Cello Suites* under his arm wherever he went. My task was to sit in a windowless office the size of a phone booth and call customers to remind them that their pianos ached for a tuning. I drummed up some business, but several of his clients were deceased or had sold their pianos. One day, I decided I'd rather pluck lice off a monkey than call another sullen piano owner. It was time to say goodbye.

During my temp agency phase, I worked the night shift at a cosmetic factory applying stickers to lipstick tubes. The conveyor belt of never-ending cylinders would have made a Buddhist anxious. Worse yet, I had to carry all my belongings in a clear plastic purse, tampon anyone. I know it was necessary, but it was demeaning. I earned a few bucks, but my newfound respect for factory workers was the actual gain.

After that stint, I told the agency I would prefer office jobs, and they sent me to work as a receptionist. Aside from answering the phone, I alphabetized paper documents and filed them in metal cabinets. Why? Back then, Silicon Valley was farmland, Bill Gates was brainstorming beside his lawnmower, and Wozniak and Jobs were picking apples.

Odd jobs are like fortune cookies. They taste like cardboard, but their message strengthens the spirit.

I See You

Every day before dinner, I traipse down the basement stairs, mount the stationary bike parked in the cold, dank workout room, and turn on the television. It takes about a mile to boot up. I watch the news because nothing generates adrenaline like politics. On days when affairs of state become unbearable, I'll reclaim my sanity and go for a spin on the beach with hermit crabs and feral horses. The stunning cinematography in nature documentaries is awe-inspiring, while the inferior quality of live-stream interviews on major news networks is baffling. Living rooms around the globe have replaced traditional studios, and a surprising number of people seem comfortable expressing themselves in garbled speech. I can only say, call your mom and let her do a sound check because she will give it to you straight, "Snookums, you sound like you're talking from inside an aquarium."

Suppose an international news channel called me and requested a live video appearance. In that case, I'd spend some time ironing the bugs out of the system. And bandwidth matters unless you don't mind sounding like you have a typewriter stuck in your throat. Video conferencing companies have troubleshooting pages, support teams, and links to the community. They want you to succeed.

And yes, camera angles can make or break your show. Yesterday, a politician spoke to his computer from the most unappealing angle. It was good that I was riding my bike and not eating because that man's distasteful face filled the entire screen. His funhouse mirror appearance and tall talk were perfect companions. What's more, his eyes bulged as he assured me that his party was improving my life. I lashed out at the set, "Nostrils are not engaging unless you're an ear, nose, and throat doctor. Pull back your chair!"

Then there are the backgrounds. Individuals attempting a scholarly appearance often record in front of bookshelves. Books do provide an intelligent-looking backdrop unless your cat happens to be licking his genitals while lounging atop your *Principles of Virology* tome.

Regardless, the award goes to the interviewee with a bazooka growing out of his ear. A large gun was parked in the man's living room, and because of the weapon's position behind his chair, the barrel appeared to be growing out of his head. I stopped listening and began wondering whether it held a subliminal message or was merely a decorating faux pas. At some point, I realized his rocket launcher was actually a telescope.

Recently, a Nobel laureate shared his wisdom from a rickety chair in front of his buttercup yellow refrigerator, an appliance from a bygone era. It wasn't surprising that his mouth and words were out of sync. At least we know he didn't upgrade his kitchen or his computer with the prize money.

Next up: a pale, sixty-ish female diplomat clad in a mustard yellow blazer. Sweetie, that color only works on a bratwurst. By the way, the teapot behind you appears to be perched on your shoulder. In case you didn't know, you can purchase a backdrop online for less than twenty dollars. There's a vast selection.

Fashion norms are eroding quicker than you can say, I think I'll fly to Cleveland in my pajamas. You may have noticed that showing off bra straps is all the rage. Speaking of bosoms, if you are endowed with mammaries to feed a city, do not opt to go au naturel under a see-through, too-tight shirt. A little jewelry enhances a look, but too much makes you look like a Christmas tree. Michael Jordan may find dangling basketball hoops attractive on a woman. I think I'll pass. And what if those earrings catch on something, they could tear an earlobe. Can torn earlobes be stitched? Boxer Mike would know the answer to that.

Oversized jewelry can look artsy or make you look like an alpine cow. Come to think of it, those poor bovines must really suffer under the weight of that big dangling bell. I've never found pierced noses on people or cattle attractive. In my quest for beauty, I avoid Little Bo-Peep ruffles and bohemian floral tops. They do not look cute or sexy on matronly women. If you are twenty and look like Barbie, you can wear anything you want or absolutely nothing at all.

Windblown hair is not always flattering on television. Likewise, brushing away annoying strands or whipping them into place with an erratic head jerk is very distracting. And when it comes to asymmetrical hairstyles, I'm never quite sure whether they're intentional or not. That type of cut must look pricey and not like your mom did it in the kitchen. On the flip side, you don't have to choose between long or short hair; you can have both.

Video chats aren't for me. I don't want to be seen when talking; I want to iron shirts and peel potatoes. I also prefer to be invisible, so I can roll my eyes and shake my head. To say nothing of indulging in lengthy conversations dressed in a bathrobe and pink hair rollers.

I'd like to mention that it's a pleasure to hear crisp, clear words traveling over wires. Maybe we're constantly texting since lousy cell phone reception makes talking exhausting. Back when phones existed solely for speaking, I never had to begin a conversation with, "Hello, can you hear me?" In fact, when I use a conventional, albeit old-fashioned home phone, I don't have to run around the house frantically searching for a hotspot. A smartphone's worst quality seems to be the phone. All the same, I understand the allure of digital communication devices. They're akin to religion for many. I have merely chosen to excommunicate myself.

Do It Yourself

It was New Year's Day, and I was stuffing a chicken when my husband entered the kitchen and asked for a sewing needle. A first, I might add.

"For what?"

"To repair my violin bow."

Believe it or not, we named our twins violin and bow. Besides ensuring their safety, we cater to their temperature and humidity needs. The one thing I thought Key would never do is fiddle, my apologies, with his bow.

After we bought a house, we became the Jack and Jill of all trades. The problem is that we cannot differentiate between projects we should handle ourselves and those we should leave to professionals. Enthusiasm clouds our judgment, and overconfidence eclipses common sense. We also tend to overestimate our abilities and underestimate the time needed to accomplish a task.

A violin bow weighs about as much as a cooked egg and can cost as much as a Lamborghini. It's difficult to imagine, but if you want a nineteenth-century bow made by Peccatte, that's what you have to pay. You can repair a crack in a violin, and it will retain most of its value. If you break a bow, you're in big trouble. It's worthless. So, a do-it-yourself bow repair made about as much sense as writing a love letter to the Mona Lisa.

I brought my sewing box into the living room, where my spouse sat comfortably on the couch, cradling the bow between his knees.

"That's probably not your best bow."

"No, it's not."

I opened the box, and he plucked a ridiculously large needle from the magnetic pin cushion.

"You could truss an ostrich with that thing. Be careful."

What more superfluous advice can anyone give? You might as well tell a person to keep breathing.

Moments later, the repairman limped into the kitchen, muttering incoherently before slumping into a chair.

"You look awful. Did you break the bow?"

"No, I broke the needle. Half of it is lodged under my kneecap, and the other half is on the couch."

"We're going to the hospital. I'll be ready in a few minutes."

I called around the neighborhood to see whether anyone could watch our eight-year-old son. In fact, friends down the street were delighted to include our child in their circus outing, so we dropped him off on our way to the clinic.

The emergency room was strangely empty, although it was undoubtedly packed the night before. Germans spend outrageous sums on pyrotechnics every New Year's Eve. And sure, lawmakers realize that a few limbs must be sacrificed in pursuit of substantial revenue, but what the heck are prosthetics for. One year, a helicopter landed in the field behind our house. We grabbed our jackets and trudged through the snow to the scene of the accident. A child on a stretcher was being loaded into the aircraft while the remainder of the team searched for the boy's finger with flashlights. I'm not permitted to mow the lawn on a Sunday, yet I'm allowed to play with dismembering rockets in my yard.

Despite being deserted, the hospital waiting room lived up to its name. I paged through magazines laced with bacteria until an orderly appeared and wheeled my husband away. An hour later, the doctor rewarded us with half a sewing needle. The staff was unfazed. I suppose emergency room doctors are used to pulling stray bits of metal out of hard-to-reach places.

Let's face it, fixing things is rewarding, and old houses are the playground of every do-it-yourselfer. We bought a house past its prime and eagerly embarked on a journey of home repair. No project was too daunting. Key installed tiles, and I grouted them with a pastry bag. We ripped off layers of anaglypta wallpaper, which was like peeling an apple with your fingers. One year, I gripped a paint roller so vigorously that I needed a cortisone shot to hold a hairbrush. After decades of heavy lifting, my husband required three spinal injections to walk like a *Homo erectus* again.

Without a doubt, home improvement projects ravage your body, but why hire a handyman when you own tools and a stack of how-to books? Over time, YouTube tutorials replaced our home repair library. Although chatty tutors who swagger onto the set wearing muscle shirts and flashing 'I love me' smiles are not encouraging my arthritic thumb up. All I can say is, *Installing Drywall* won't win you an Oscar, so please stop babbling and get to the point.

Time and again, we were seduced by the broken, the scratched, and the battered. Therefore, I wasn't surprised when my spouse decided it was time to install a radiator in one of our basement rooms. One Saturday morning, he drove to a nearby plumbing supply store and bought a radiator and matching pipes. Then, after hours of hammering and sawing, he invited me into the basement to see our new addition. I was impressed, but before turning to go upstairs, I noticed a trickle.

"I think the elbow pipe is leaking."

"I hope not."

"Sorry, the joint is definitely dripping," I said, pointing.

"Maybe the pipe is sweating. It might be condensed water."

"It's dripping, not sweating."

"Yeah, I know. I was just hoping that it wasn't."

I would have hurled expletives at the pipe, but he simply looked downtrodden.

"Do you need any help?"

"No, there's nothing you can do."

I went upstairs, and an hour later, he called me back into the basement.

Cringing, I stared at the newly installed pipe. "You see it, don't you? There's a gash in the adjacent pipe. And it's dripping."

His face blanched. He touched the pipe, and it was wet.

"I must have nicked it with the electric saw."

"Is it necessary to drain the water from the system again?"

"I can't. I'm out of replacement pipes, and the plumbing store is closed."

"Now what?"

"I need a bucket."

In do-it-yourself land, the mental anguish inflicted by previous ventures is soon forgotten. A new project is always in the works.

A few years ago, while browsing around a dimly lighted, overcrowded antique shop reeking of mold, we found the perfect cabinet for our bathroom. However, its countless layers of paint and cracked varnish needed to be removed. The shop owner suggested we have it dipped in a vat of solvent. Naturally, I declined. Where's the thrill and the challenge in that?

We made the purchase, flattened the car's seats, and tried not to tear the ceiling's upholstery as we pushed the ugly duckling inside our vehicle. I justified the undertaking by telling myself how much money I was saving by doing this myself.

The following morning, I spent an absurd amount on brushes, scrapers, sandpaper, stripper fluid, and a heat gun. With Key's help, I covered the terrace with newspapers and moved the cabinet outside. Then, the wise man left for work.

Wearing rubber gloves, I pried open the hazardous can of stripper and applied the toxic liquid to the wood. Bubbles were supposed to appear in the paint, making it easy to scrape off, but it turned gooey instead. The cabinet looked like it had been ravaged by pestilence. After a single swipe, the scraper was coated in gunk. Thirty minutes later, I berated myself for not having the cabinet dipped.

I abandoned the liquid stripper and plugged in the electric heat gun. I would like to point out that heat guns are designed to strip untouched paint, not to remove goo. As the sludge got hot, I smeared it like cake icing and left burn marks on the wood that are still visible. Using my newly acquired wire brush, I attempted to scrub off the slime but gouged the wood and mucked up the brush.

How does one strip grooves and indentations? You send your furniture to be dipped in a special liquid and returned to you paint-free. I closed the stripper can, threw my grimy rubber gloves onto the newspaper, and unplugged the heat gun. That evening, over a bottle of red wine, Key suggested I try sanding the cabinet.

Before leaving for orchestra rehearsal the next day, he placed an electric sander, and a box filled with various strengths of sandpaper on the kitchen table.

Feeling rejuvenated and freshly motivated, I began sanding, effectively transforming yesterday's sludge into sticky dust. After a few breaths of toxic grime, I realized it might be a good idea to put on the goggles and face mask my husband had set on the table. With each passing hour, the loathing I felt for the cabinet grew.

"I detest you!" I cried.

"I have a confession to make. I have worms."

"What did you just say?"

"My wood is wormy. I'll be chewed to a pile of dust in a few years."

"You tricked me."

"Antiques are tricky, but you knew that."

"Oh, just shut your drawer. And by the way, I refuse to massage you with scented oil after all the anguish you've caused me."

"That's your husband's forte, and I'm sure he'll make me look lovely."

"Knock on wood, maggot lover."

Around the age of fifty, the desire to do it myself waned, and the thrill I once felt morphed into inertia. Nowadays, I'm not in the mood to paint, grout tiles, or sew curtains. In any case, my passion for baking remains, so I think I'll wrap this up and head to the kitchen. But first, I'll grab the ladder and harvest a few apples from our overgrown tree. Oh well, as long as I'm up there, I might as well prune the damned thing.

On the Road

While stuck in traffic last week, I barely noticed the three-wheeled vehicle in front of me. I'm talking about a morsel of an automobile from the previous century, not some stunning futuristic electric car. It was certainly the kind of thing that you only see in Europe. An elderly man sat inside, probably a small man judging by the car's size. Hitting a squirrel would have sent his tricycle into a spin, and I don't mean this in a derogatory way. Tiny cars, like tiny houses, often have a toy-like quality.

The three-wheeler had a sunroof, but the latch was inconveniently positioned behind the man's head. When traffic was at a standstill, he struggled to open the window. Once we started moving, he fumbled to close it. This caused the car to careen around the road in a zigzag pattern like a fleeing rabbit. Even though I didn't have a pressing appointment, I still mumbled a snide remark about driving impaired people.

My question is, why do we turn into fire-breathing dragons as soon as we pull out of the garage? Primordial feelings churn in our guts, then rise up the vagus nerve to our brains, making us scorn the mediocrity and ineptness of those around us. Let's face it, the high standard of our own driving is unrivaled. Although, in this case, I felt slightly guilty about my misanthropic rant. What goes around comes around, and before long, I will be an insecure old lady in a polyester jogging outfit, pitifully attempting to maneuver my shopping cart.

But nothing, I mean absolutely nothing I've experienced on any road, comes close to the high-spirited, perilous ride I underwent in India. We were adopting a child from an orphanage in the middle of the subcontinent. A six-hour drive separated her village from the airport where I was landing. I was uptight about my husband traveling with me, and insisted he stay home with our son. "What if the plane crashes or we're killed in a car accident? Then both kids would be orphans," I said.

Early in the adoption process, through a mutual acquaintance, we became email friends with a family from our daughter's village. Despite never having met the father, he hired a car and accompanied the driver on the six-hour trek to meet me at the airport. After we introduced ourselves, we got into the car. About twenty hair-raising minutes into the trip, it soon became clear that the odds were against survival. Haphazard does not even begin to describe the choreography of the road. Tailgating is the norm, but seatbelts are not. And close calls are a quintessential part of the journey. Speed limits are unnecessary because the pace is determined by the situation. Drivers stop abruptly for cows. Ancient Ta Ta trucks whiz past rickshaws powered by skinny legs, and vehicles of all shapes and sizes in various stages of decay share the road with cattle and pedestrians. Incessant honking exacerbates the bubbling salmagundi. Marked lanes are superfluous since everyone just squeezes in wherever they can. Never once did I glimpse a turn signal. At least they don't wave with their middle fingers or shoot each other.

Roads are dangerous. It's what they have in common everywhere in the world. Recently, my brother-in-law was a victim of road rage. While crossing a New Jersey street, a car came racing around the corner and grazed him. The driver, being an exemplary human being, stopped in the middle of the road and got out of his car to ensure he was okay. No, he did not. He punched him in the face, then casually drove off. You never know when you will encounter a person with the social graces of a crocodile.

Indeed, the purring of a car can be a source of pleasure. Sad to say, I venerate our car about as much as our vacuum cleaner. Owning a luxury vehicle is pointless for us. Not only is the price a deterrent, but our narrow European garage has made a hobby of amputating side mirrors. If we drove a classy car, I would get emotional every time the pole in the parking lot rammed our rear bumper. Repairing a dent in our Corolla is expensive enough, but imagine the tab for fixing a luxury car's boo-boo.

In the seventies, I was content moseying along the highways of America at a fuel-efficient 55 mph. A drowsy pace is eco-friendly and conducive to arriving at your destination alive. I live in Germany and don't need to keep up with the Fritzes. The way I see it, the autobahn is for the fearless. Quite a few drivers are intoxicated by speed. Not me. The equivalent of six hundred and fifty horses barreling down on me makes me feel like I'm being chased to the grave, and it is particularly frightening when the bright red beast flashes its headlights at my bumper. This is known as *drängeln* and means move over now. Tailgating is foolish and deadly. Environmental groups have been calling for an autobahn speed limit for years, but leading German automakers fear tempo restrictions will dampen their revenue, although robust global sales suggest otherwise. A quick word to car manufacturers: countries enforcing speed limits are buying fast German cars faster than ever.

A few years ago, while taking a family vacation in the American West, I said to my husband, "You've been doing most of the driving. Let me take over for a while." Relieved, he handed me the keys. I don't know who regrets that move more.

I pulled out of the Yosemite parking lot and onto a street flanked by trees. We feasted on splendid scenery for about three miles before the forest ended. Suddenly, I found myself hugging the rim of a rocky canyon. There was nothing between us and a bottomless abyss. Did somebody forget to build a guardrail? Doesn't a sheer drop justify some type of barrier? Even a perfunctory railing would have prevented me from drowning in a cocktail of fight-or-flight hormones. Hairpin curves significantly elevated my adrenaline, and I imagined our car cascading over the edge and dangling precariously from a rocky outcrop until we were rescued and brought safely back to my parents' house in Ohio, where, at this moment, I wish we had stayed. My behavior must have frightened my family because they were very still.

"Why don't you let me drive," Key suggested.

"There's nowhere to pull over," I shrieked.

As I crept around the bends, I became increasingly overwrought. Miles of cars cruised quietly behind me. "My nerves are shot, and the people trailing me know it. Otherwise, they would be honking."

A scenic viewpoint up the road put an end to my misery. I pulled over, tumbled out of the car, and gave the brooding drivers behind me a chance to gawk.

Someday, I will ride around in a marvel of technology that drives itself. And there's a good chance the vehicle will relish being in the driver's seat more than I do.

Cord to Camera

My mother breezed through the mornings of my childhood perched on a red vintage milk can with the phone braced between her ear and shoulder. In one hand, she cradled a glass of orange juice, and in the other, she twirled the phone's cord like a jump rope. No sooner had she finished her juice than she was eager for the first blissful smoke of the day. A Salem. She tapped a cigarette from its kelly green box, lit it, then stubbed it out after a few gratifying puffs. Half-smoked cigarettes invariably belonged to her morning conversations, which were like sporting events, complete with shouting, cheering, and skirmishes. Unfolding crises provided suspenseful storylines; much ado about nothing comes to mind. My mother was partial to wearing a bathrobe for her emotionally charged morning news. I sat at the table, crunching sugary cereal while pretending not to be glued to the music of her fervent discussions.

Growing up, I shared the phone with four siblings and my parents. My father engaged in low-key, laconic conversations, whereas my mother's sessions were long and fiery. Whenever she was steeped in conversation and I had an important call to make, such as making plans with my friends, I raised my eyebrows like a despondent puppy. Predictably, she replied with her just a minute finger. Sometimes, she wrapped it up, but when she kept right on chatting, I stated my case on paper and stood before her begging like a hungry drifter. Siblings tying up the phone were a different story. Our silent bickering was Chaplinesque; hands-on-hips, I planted myself in front of the caller and huffed loudly. A scowl followed. Minutes later, gritting my teeth, I marched back into the room, furiously tapping my left wrist.

We continued our theatrical displays of affection until I went to college, where communal living meant, yet again, a communal phone. Only this time, it was a payphone mounted in the dorm hallway. These days, people would share a face mask before sharing a phone.

I was born into a world of olive-green rotary phones. Dialing had a hypnotic charm and couldn't be rushed. You inserted your index finger into a hole in the rotary wheel and propelled it around a plate until it hit a crescent-shaped finger stopper. While waiting for the dial to return, you had time to ponder existential questions, like whether the neighbors would eavesdrop on your forthcoming conversation. My parents didn't pay extra for an individual service line, and listening in was irresistible and pretty much expected.

Communication devices sprinted up technology's evolutionary ladder, and it wasn't long before a stylish push-button phone adorned our kitchen. Adieu, party line. Farewell, dialing. Hello, tuneful buttons. There's more to come, there always is. Shortly after, cordless phones summoned us to the cash register, erasing my mother's cord gymnastics forever. Finally, free from the phone's restricting leash, she could roam the house while chatting.

In no time, my mother had phones installed on every floor. "Why climb a flight of stairs," she mused, "when you can have extensions," as they were called in the eighties. Multiple devices eliminated the athletics of running to the kitchen to answer the phone, and one was never out of breath for that first sweet hello.

My family never procrastinated when it came to shopping, and as soon as answering machines hit the shelves, we rushed to the mall. That accessory quenched a thirst I never knew my mother had; she simply had to know the identity of the person who opted not to leave a message. The moment she walked in the door, she was drawn to the blinking red light like a moth to a bulb. First, she waded through the hang-ups, chiding callers who refused to speak to the machine. Oh yes, she knew who they were because their numbers flashed on the display. Then she listened to the messages. The fact that she prioritized the uncommunicative callers always baffled me because not all phone calls have a purpose; therefore, callers do not always need to leave a message. Essentially, answering machines were the first devices to identify us without our consent. A feature, I might add, that evolved into a nightmarish roller coaster ride pretty damn quick.

Tele and phone form the rather poetic expression meaning distant voice in Greek. Long before Alexander Graham Bell patented his telephone in 1876, people lusted after telecommunication devices. Our phone craving could have been satisfied thirty years earlier had Innocenzo Manzetti, an Italian native, patented his speaking telegraph or, at the very least, shown his invention to fellow scientists. While Manzetti was sipping Campari on the piazza, Alexander Bell skipped down the yellow brick road to commercial success. Before the arrival of the phone, society communicated by telegraph. Ironically, during Bell's phone demonstration, many thought it unnecessary to hear a person's voice when you could just send a telegram. We have come full circle.

In the not too distant future, every earthling's pocket would be ringing. Meanwhile, phone booths were our phones away from home. I can assure you that the phone company could have cared less about your location or shopping habits. Callers left that booth without a trace unless they shoved a wad of chewing gum into the coin return or spilled their sticky coke on the floor. Standing in the middle of a city inside a narrow glass box and dropping a coin in the slot was a gratifying experience. Most booths provided a user-friendly, six-pound phone directory. Suppose a delinquent stole or hacked up the book; you simply dialed zero, and a human being not named Siri said, "Operator speaking, how may I help you?" In the 1970s, the phone book slogan was: *Let your fingers do the walking*. Thumbs up to that.

One Christmas, Santa brought the whole world cell phones, and now we can talk anytime, anywhere. Occasionally, I step off the subway scratching my head, not on account of picking up lice but because I unwillingly know the dramatic saga of a complete stranger's life. Some people don't seem to mind sharing their lives with an audience, even while utilizing a public toilet stall. I feel vulnerable with my pants down, and besides, I refuse to answer the call of nature and the phone simultaneously. Nobody wants to listen to a draining bladder.

I've seen children too young to speak, swishing their tiny pink fingers on cell phones. Why? Because they are still sucking their thumbs. My entire life, I have dialed phones with my index finger. My thumbs are neither capable nor enthusiastic tappers. My son claims that dialing a smartphone with an index finger is something that only old people do. That is correct.

Phones aren't really phones anymore, are they? They are seductive little computers that nurture our need to know, drive our inclination to judge (like, follow, share), and satisfy our ravenous appetite to preserve the humdrum alongside the spectacular. Our information sponge is never truly saturated. Fortunately, being connected is not a privilege; the poor and the wealthy are digital equals. And we are both masters and servants of the phone. Can you hear me?

Flying

We were on our way out the door to catch a flight from Munich to Toronto when I noticed that my eleven-year-old son was wearing flip-flops. "What if we have to evacuate the plane? Do you want to risk walking on fire and broken glass in a thong sandal?" I spouted. "Try sliding down the inflatable escape slide in floppy shoes. And besides, they look slovenly for traveling abroad. Maybe the ancient Greeks wore sandals to the theater, but they didn't risk a sprained ankle while running to catch their connecting flight." My son put on his sneakers halfway through the rant.

Our annual flight to Cleveland usually included a layover in Philadelphia. Not anymore. After September 11th, I was apprehensive about flying to an East Coast airport and felt more comfortable passing through Toronto. Travel was no longer about enjoyment; it was about vigilance. In the months following the World Trade Center attacks, on a flight from Paris to Miami, a man attempted to detonate bombs concealed in the heels of his shoes. Thanks to him, unhappily ever after, we must remove our shoes, jackets, and belts for screening. As for sandals, all I can say is I hope you don't mind walking barefoot on floors contaminated with pathogens from around the world.

A few days before our flight, I watched a riveting documentary about surviving a plane crash. For instance, I learned you should never inflate your life jacket before exiting an aircraft. Like most people, I assumed an inflated vest would take up too much space. The fact is, if your malfunctioning airliner is forced to make a water landing and you inflate your jacket inside the cabin, the rising water will thrust you and your puffed-up vest up to the ceiling, and you will drown. To drive the point home, the film reenacted tragic stories of passengers pinned to overhead compartments. One especially horrific scene depicted a young girl struggling to free her grandmother from the inflated death trap. To no avail, I might add. It blows my mind that flight attendants never mention this during the pre-flight safety talk. In my book, knowing that your flotation device can both save and kill you is essential information. Ignorance is not bliss. Sometimes you need to understand the rationale behind a regulation to prepare yourself for an emergency before it occurs.

As we approached Toronto, an Air France plane overshot the runway, crashed into a creek near the airport, and burst into flames. The passengers and crew had ninety seconds to escape. Miraculously, everyone survived. "Probably because nobody was wearing flip-flops," I said to my son.

Meanwhile, back home in Germany, breaking news interrupted Key's television program to show a story about the Toronto crash, which occurred moments before our scheduled landing. In an era when fewer than half of the population owned cell phones, myself included, I couldn't reach him until I disembarked.

After getting off the plane, we waited in line to use the phone. I'm surprised that pay phones weren't obsolete by the time it was our turn. First, I called Key and then my parents, who were expecting us in Cleveland that evening. My mother picked up on the second ring. "Mom, we're fine, but we're not getting out of here tonight. I have to go. Hordes of people need to use the phone. No, don't drive to Toronto. I'll call you after I rebook."

Clearly, he who hesitates sleeps on a dirty airport floor. I grabbed my son and ran to the hotel booking desk. As expected, the line was the length of a football field. When we finally reached the front, the clerk informed me that the airport hotel had already sold out.

"I have a child with me. We'll sleep anywhere, even in a linen closet. Please check again."

She pounded the keys and smiled. "There's a room with wet carpeting. The rug was shampooed today, and it isn't dry yet."

"I'd give my eyeteeth for that room."

"A credit card will do," the nice lady said.

The following summer, our flight to Cleveland was uneventful. But a year later, terrorists plotted to blow up transatlantic flights using liquid explosives disguised as soft drinks. British and US intelligence agencies squelched the plot before any planes went down. I remember standing in the middle of my parents' living room watching thousands of confiscated water, lotion, liquor, and soft drink bottles pile up at the airport. Transportation security had banned passengers from carrying on, as they put it, all nonsolid forms of matter. I surely couldn't fly back to Germany without hand lotion, and placed a single-use foil pouch of moisturizer between the pages of my book, then patted myself on the back with remarkably soft hands.

Apparently, flying is safer than driving. Maybe our brains cling to statistics, but our guts don't. Flying makes me jumpy, so I take a beta-blocker before boarding a plane. Let me tell you, this magic pill blocks the receptors for adrenaline and other stress hormones without making you drowsy. Beta-blockers may ease anxiety, but they don't curb the irritation that plagues me when I'm forced to travel beside an annoying person.

In lieu of pills, some travelers rely on emotional support animals to tame the butterflies in their stomachs. I wish I owned a creature that could calm my fears and nip irritating people. A woman once attempted to board a plane with her emotional support peacock. As you can imagine, her feathered friend was denied entry. Astonishingly, another carrier permitted a turkey to escort a passenger. Maybe it's time for the airlines to tackle avian discrimination. While they're at it, perhaps they could stop serving overcooked chicken on international flights.

My flying fantasy is to have an entire row to myself, but if I must have a seatmate, a cello would make an ideal companion. Professional musicians flying with pricey cellos have it rough. They will never check them into the cargo hold, and those who wish to bring their instrument into the cabin must purchase a seat.

Once, a friend was traveling with his cello and had just settled into his seat when a flight attendant tapped him on the shoulder and said, "I'm sorry, sir, this is an emergency exit row, and unfortunately, your cello cannot stay here."

"But my cello has a ticket."

"A cello cannot assist others in an emergency. I'll be right back."

The flight attendant returned moments later. "I have good news, there's a seat available for your instrument in first class."

"Can I have its meal?"

Speaking of carry-on luggage, since airlines began charging for checked bags, the overhead bins are stuffed to bursting, and you have a fat chance of getting any bin space when you board in zone five. You must pay for a boarding zone upgrade to ensure your carry-on bag can be carried on. The skies are not friendly anymore.

Regarding snack foods on flights from Europe to the United States, I strongly advise against accepting a complimentary apple from the airline. First of all, you cannot bring it into the country, and worse, it is annoyingly crunchy. A woman recently attempted to enter the United States with an in-flight apple and was charged five hundred dollars by customs. Indeed, it is the solemn duty of border protection to keep America safe from foreign fruit, but an apple, really? The airline eschewed all responsibility and claimed the apple was meant for consumption on the flight.

At the time of writing, due to the Coronavirus, I hook the loops of a mask behind my ears before entering an airport. A loose-fitting surgical mask may be good enough for open-heart surgery, but in Germany, it does not suffice for a flight to Greece. The protective barrier I'm required to wear is heavy and hot. After the mask is securely suffocating me, I pump hand sanitizer onto my hands from a bottle near the door and vigorously rub away the germs.

Grudgingly, I stand in line behind two hundred other passengers waiting to check in. Moisture from my breath moistens the mask. I am uncomfortable. I don't like the mask and am relieved when it's nearly my turn. But the family in front of me seems to have a problem. Their suitcase is too heavy, and they need to pay for the additional weight. Did Mommy really need several pairs of shoes? Yes, she did. The airline, however, is not being nice to Mommy. They want her to pay with a credit card, but Mommy doesn't have a credit card; she has a screaming infant. Babies are not required to wear masks, so I don't know why the child is crying. Mommy's husband turns to me and asks whether I have a credit card. My response is, "I do, and yeah, I'll pay." He assures me he'll get cash from the ATM and reimburse me. I believe him. He looks honest. Well, the unmasked portion does. And then I swipe my Visa card. Frankly, I'm drained after two years of Corona restrictions and don't care whether he pays me back.

When it's my turn to check in, I show my digital Corona vaccination certificate and passport. The unvaccinated must have a swab the size of a chopstick shoved up their nostrils no later than twenty-four hours before the flight; otherwise, they cannot board the plane. I'd rather be jabbed with a needle than have a pipe cleaner repeatedly shoved up my nose. The fact is, unless you have proof of vaccination or a negative test result, it is impossible to go anywhere.

I receive my boarding pass, and as I turn around, I see Baby Daddy rushing toward me, waving the cash. He is gasping for air as he hands me the money. I smile, but of course, he doesn't see it.

On the way to the gate, I go through security. My nonsolid forms of matter are ready and waiting in a plastic bag, which I place in a gray bin along with my shoes, jacket, backpack, and phone. Then I step onto a platform for a full-body scan. A grim woman waving a hand scanner does not like my image and asks me to step aside. "Please show me what you have in your hair." I did not have lice, but I did have a little plastic hair comb wedged behind my hairline to prevent loose strands from falling on my face. I hold the comb up like a chalice, and she waves me through.

That's all, folks. I have a flight to catch.

Diagnosis

Have you ever been uncertain whether you have a cold? Probably not, but cancer isn't like that; it's a subtle predator. Something has gone awry in the recesses of your body, and by the time symptoms begin to haunt and taunt you, it's usually too late. In my case, and I say this unabashedly, constipation and diarrhea took turns tormenting me. Despite my glaring symptoms, I still had better things to do than go for a colonoscopy.

For one thing, cancer never crossed my mind. For another, I was certain that drinking coffee on an empty stomach was causing my troubles; therefore, eating an oatmeal cookie would alleviate them. I imagined the cookie absorbing the acidic irritants in coffee like an internal paper towel. The joke was on me.

After that, it occurred to me there might be a tapeworm wriggling through the maze of my viscera, so I foolishly stopped eating sushi. One day, cramps joined the party, and in my infinite wisdom, I chalked them up to lady problems. At long last, the internet diagnosed me with irritable bowel syndrome and recommended a five-star medicine. In one click, my cure was on its way.

Months later, I visited my sister in Texas and whined about my misbehaving gut.

"You need a colonoscopy."

"I'm not sure."

"Yeah, you do. By the way, you don't look too good."

"I look wretched, and do you know why? The guy sitting next to me on the plane played video games on his in-flight entertainment screen throughout the entire trip. After five thousand miles of tapping, my nerves are shot. But yeah, I should probably get the test."

Why did I avoid the colonoscopy? Because the thought of fasting and drinking a gallon of bowel-flushing liquid did not appeal to me. Unfortunately, there is no substitute for a colonoscopy. As of yet, no high-tech scan or telepathic soothsayer can accurately assess the state of your large intestine. The big guy measures five feet and must be squeaky clean for the procedure. On a side note, the twenty-foot serpent coiled beneath your stomach, known as the small intestine, is only accessible by mouth.

Upon returning to Germany, I called a local gastroenterologist. The receptionist asked my age, which was fifty-three, and whether I had a reason for requesting the test. After listening to my story, she scheduled an appointment.

Several days before the procedure, I stopped eating seeds and nuts. Cranberry juice was also off the menu because it dyes your insides crimson and can be mistaken for blood. The day before the colonoscopy, I had plain yogurt for breakfast, clear broth for lunch, and a large pitcher of laxative for dinner.

I once flushed out my vacuum cleaner hose, which ironically is about the length of a human colon, and all the gunk came gushing out. But when purging your colon, you're in for the long haul. The last time I spent that much time on the toilet was in Spain after eating aioli dip made with raw eggs. Salmonella turns your gut into a boiling cauldron of misery, and although the colonoscopy purgative hits you like a tsunami, it's comfortably purifying. Seeing as I had a plethora of bathroom cleaning tasks to choose from, I scrubbed shower tiles, polished chrome, and organized the medicine cabinet between sessions on the john.

Early the next morning, my husband drove me to the doctor. The receptionist ushered me into the dressing room and handed me a pair of one-size-fits-all paper shorts featuring a posterior hole, similar to the open crotch pants worn by Chinese toddlers. My boxer shorts, however, provided a portal to my speckless entrails and not an exit. I changed into the pants and lay down on the examination table. A nurse installed a port in my arm, and the doctor injected an anesthetic that made the ceiling spin as it whisked me away to never-never land.

Based on the fascinating YouTube video I watched the night before, *A Journey Through the Colon and Removal of*

Polyps, I knew the doctor would browse around and take pictures.

Shortly after I awoke, he said, "We removed a harmless-looking polyp, and we're sending it to pathology as a precaution."

I didn't expect him to follow the video to the letter, but I wasn't concerned either. I thanked him and went home.

A week later, the doctor called and said, "I have to see you this morning. Can you be here in an hour?"

"Do you think we could talk on the phone?"

"No, I need to speak with you in person."

Upon entering his office, I could see that he appeared anxious.

"I'm afraid that I have some unexpected news. The polyp is cancerous, but the real issue is that your tumor has grown a few millimeters into the intestinal wall."

"What does that mean?"

"It means that the lymph nodes surrounding the tumor may be cancerous, thus I highly recommend removing them. Regrettably, you will need a colostomy bag after the surgery."

"A colonoscopy. Didn't I just have that?"

"I'm referring to a colostomy bag."

"Aren't those for old people?"

"Your colon needs to be bypassed for three months to heal, but the truth is you might need the bag forever."

"Why?"

"Your tumor was in the rectum, and surgery may lead to incontinence. In which case, you'll need it permanently."

"Can't you just sew up my gut and skip the bag?"

"No, otherwise, you risk infection."

The prospect of having a colostomy bag was as unsettling as the diagnosis. I have a long life ahead of me, right? I'll have plenty of time to berate myself for avoiding the colonoscopy. When a cancerous polyp is caught before it grows into your intestinal tissue, it probably hasn't spread to other organs, and you don't need surgery. Every decision we make has consequences. If I'd gone for the colonoscopy sooner, I might have avoided the entire ordeal.

Life stops being ordinary after an alarming diagnosis, and I felt like a passenger on a downward spiraling plane. Since more tests were required, the risk of bad news increased with each exam. How concerned does the CT technician look? Is the ultrasound doctor frowning at my liver, a common first stop for colon cancer metastasis. Until now, I was unaware of the predictable routes that tumors take. Fortunately, the tests revealed disease-free organs, and by the end of the week, I was in the hospital for lymph node surgery.

My insurance company offered me a double room in the shiny new wing or a single in the old run-down area. "I'll sleep in a broom closet just to be alone," I told the administrator. After signing a dozen forms, she showed me to my room. It was shabby but clean, although you can't see germs, can you? Did you know that more harmful bacteria live on two square inches of your kitchen sponge than people who've ever lived on our planet? Undoubtedly, morbid microbes were crawling on every surface of the hospital.

I was sitting in bed staring at the chimney stacks outside my window when a cheerful colostomy nurse arrived to discuss the best spot on my abdomen for the bag. It was almost a normal conversation, like I was being fitted for a dress and not an external septic tank. She casually drew a circle on my stomach with her Sharpie and bounced out the door. Around an hour later, a no-nonsense lady hugging a clipboard entered my room. She handed me a list of pre-surgical exams and said, "You are scheduled for a few tests this afternoon, and you have an appointment with the anesthesiologist at four. Do you have any questions?"

"Nope."

The building reminded me of a parking garage as I navigated the maze of unadorned concrete hallways to my first exam. The door was ajar when I arrived, and I peeked around the corner. A friendly nurse invited me in, asked me to sign a few forms, and then gave me a pair of paper pants.

"You can change in there," she said, pointing at a door.

"This is not what I expected. Am I having another colonoscopy?" I asked.

"No, we need to determine the location of the tumor that was removed during your colonoscopy."

"Will I be anesthetized?"

"That isn't necessary, the procedure won't take long."

After changing into the pants, I entered the examination room. The doctor arrived carrying a pipe etched with lines and numbers. It resembled a prop from a mafia movie. My nerves got the better of me.

"Please lie down on the table and turn onto your left side. This will be uncomfortable," he warned.

I held my breath as he maneuvered the pipe through my constricted sphincter muscle. He probed around, and at irregular intervals, his assistant pumped air up the tube into my colon. Blindsided by pain, I grasped the sheet. "Are we nearly finished?" I bleated.

"This is proving to be more difficult than expected. It shouldn't take much longer."

I feigned tolerance, but the procedure was an unyielding, physical storm. After it was over, I hobbled away, browbeating myself, yet again, for avoiding the colonoscopy.

Hunched over and dazed, I found the anesthesiologist's office. He suggested pairing anesthesia with an epidural to avoid pain after waking. "I'd rather pair it with a Cabernet. Sorry, I don't want an obscenely long needle inserted into my spine. The fact is, I once had an epidural that caused me nearly a year of back pain." After signing more forms, I returned to my room.

A nurse entered carrying a pitcher of bowel-flushing liquid. She set the beverage and a cup on the table and said, "You have to drink it all, but you can take your time." An hour later, I was in the bathroom. Strange toilets can be unappealing, but I've used campsite restrooms that were more praiseworthy than this lavatory. I don't want to seem ungrateful because I felt only gratitude toward my surgeon and the hospital. Nevertheless, I'm a clean freak, which makes me particularly fault-finding regarding bathrooms.

"Rise and shine," a bubbly orderly chirped as he released the brakes on my bed and wheeled me to a preoperative holding area. After a brief chat with the staff, it was time for surgery.

The next thing I remember is waking up in the recovery room. A nurse noticed my stirring and brought me a mug of warm herbal tea, the beverage of choice in German hospitals. Essential oils wafted up from the cup and churned my stomach. "I'm sorry, I can't drink that." She put down the mug and showed me how to operate the morphine pump. Regrettably, the well-known opiate didn't relieve the pain or improve my mood.

Still lightheaded from the anesthetic, I ran my finger along the staples running down the center of my abdomen. They seemed unnecessarily hefty for closing delicate skin and more appropriate for upholstering leather. Warily, I patted the colostomy bag and thought, this is your first toilet sabbatical since you were an embryo. Then, I headed north to probe the needle in my neck, which was more or less a pain in the neck. Under the covers, I found dual drainage tubes and a catheter, which meant I didn't require a toilet for anything whatsoever. I turned my attention back to the bag, naïve to the fact that I would soon loathe this sack with a vengeance.

That night, cold, wet sheets woke me up. Lo-and-behold, blood was leaking from the nether side of the bag. I pressed the call button, and a nurse came to assess the situation. "You need a doctor," she said.

Moments later, a young female MD arrived to fix the leak. She removed the pouch, and I was stunned to see a writhing worm sutured to my stomach.

"Excuse me, I thought there would be a hole in my abdomen?"

"That's part of your small intestine, otherwise known as the stoma."

"Well, it sure has a mind of its own."

My entrail stretched and contracted. Had this little section of viscera not been sewn in place, it would have squirmed out of my body. Unbelievably, my small intestine did its job, undeterred by the new circumstances. As I pondered my innards, the doctor reached for a fish-hook-shaped needle.

"How about some anesthetic?"

"A numbing injection would hurt more than the stitches."

I looked away and pressed my poppy pump for good measure.

The doctor completed her needlework, and the nurse reattached my pouch.

Incidentally, stoma is the Greek word for mouth. Foul mouth would be more appropriate. Sea anemones have mouths resembling stomas, but the ancient Greeks were fond of opium and cannabis and probably named things while high.

Occasionally, my son filled his diaper while nursing, and like everything he did, I thought it was adorable. But there was nothing cute about my stoma broadcasting the digestive progress at the dinner table.

Several days after surgery, I learned that the lymph nodes were not cancerous. The news should have put me in seventh heaven. Honestly, I wasn't in the mood for heaven, seventh or otherwise. Adjusting to life with a colostomy bag and a skewed digestive system corroded my spirit and knocked me completely out of alignment.

According to Wikipedia, modern pouching systems allow people to resume normal activities after surgery without physical evidence of the stoma or the pouching system. I'd wager the author of this article never had a bag running rampant with excrement bulging from his side. A popular stoma blog claimed you could wear everything you wore before. Sure, if an oversized poncho belonged to your fashion statement, then yes, by all means, dig it out and slip it on.

I'd like to ask you to stop reading for a minute, grab a balloon, fill it with warm water, and duct tape it to your midriff. What do you think? Is your outfit looking good? Are you feeling pretty? Does that big pendulous object affect your apparel's appearance? But remember, your balloon is filled with clean water, and mine isn't.

As soon as I popped a tasty morsel into my mouth, I had about twelve minutes before the stoma started percolating and spurting its brew. Metamucil slammed on the brakes by transforming the contents of my small intestine into a gelatinous glob. Which was great until stomach acid leaked from the stoma, causing the skin of my abdomen to dissolve. Vaseline soothed the owie but prevented the receptacle from adhering to my body.

During the three months I had the bag, I emptied it around fifteen times a day, or one hundred and five times a week. The bag was always warm, which also made it feel wet. Then, one day, I was out shopping, and my little parcel of fecal matter suddenly felt different. "Just relax," I said to myself. Clearly, my sensible self knew better and yelled, "Get to the bathroom, you fool. Your anxiety is justified!"

Indeed, the ring had disconnected, and the bag was leaking. For openers, shit happens, so I decided early on to carry the colostomy paraphernalia with me at all times. Furthermore, the horrible creature spurts like Old Faithful while you replace its bits and pieces, so you must tuck a trash bag into your pants to avoid making a mess. The routine was terribly stressful. Let me say that again, minus the euphemism. It was repulsive.

The day for the reversal had finally arrived. In other words, it was time to remove the vile bag and reunite my small intestine with its bowel mate. I couldn't wait to get to the hospital.

Upon waking from surgery, I celebrated by drinking the herbal tea the wake-up nurse offered me. And this time, the kidney shaped metal basin beside my pillow was put to excellent use. I'd like to take a moment to apologize to my wake-up mates, for those thin curtain dividers do not reduce sounds.

Two days later, I went home, eager to eat and excrete the old-fashioned way. Soon, it became apparent that every morsel had to be tested near a bathroom. Never before had peanuts, tomatoes, and fibrous vegetables sent me running. Now they did.

The surgeon constructed an internal pocket to give me a few extra seconds to reach the facilities. However, the bathroom could be only a stone's throw away. In Europe, public restrooms are about as rare as snow in Texas, so leaving the house induced fear and anxiety. The year after the colostomy reversal, I didn't go to restaurants because the drive home would have been too risky. When I absolutely had to go out, I fasted beforehand and popped an Imodium.

Within a month of the reversal, I embarked on a family vacation to Venice, which I had foolishly booked before the surgery. Traveling for six minutes was already stressful. How would I cope for six hours? The morning of our trip, I had Imodium for breakfast and tossed a blanket in the trunk in case I needed an emergency outhouse. Nobody would be the wiser if I dashed into a field and threw it over my head. They would undoubtedly wonder, but they would never know what was happening underneath that quilt.

By the way, food takes one to three days to pass through the digestive tract. However, when Imodium is added to the mix, your overactive intestines become sluggish and unpredictable, meaning the floodgates can open at any moment.

In Venice, my family indulged in Italian delicacies, and I nibbled on white bread and cheese. We require about a thousand calories a day to keep the machinery running: heart, lungs, intestines, and brain. Any vestige of shame vanishes during a physical emergency, but can you imagine using the Grand Canal as a toilet? I ate only enough to survive.

It was a sweltering day, and copious gelato stands challenged my willpower. "I am buying a scoop of ice cream," I told my family. Once again, the rational part of my brain tried to ruin my fun. "Do you think that's a good idea? You've heard things about bacteria in ice cream. Look around. It's all sitting out in the sun." I'm googling this. *The Chilling Truth* popped up first and discussed oils, fillers, and whipped air in ice cream. That makes for some scary dairy, yet the information wasn't relevant to my situation. In the middle of a crowded Venetian piazza, I searched for a solution to my dilemma and came across *Bacteria in Ice Cream*. After reading about the perils lurking in contaminated gelato, I reached into my purse for a cracker.

My gut was holding me hostage, and I was fed up with its wayward conduct. In my quest to improve digestion, I bought a bottle of mud harvested from the bottom of a peat bog. I drank the recommended dosage for a few days and discovered that bog mud is better suited as a face mask. Brewer's yeast gave no discernible relief, nor did the pectin in vegan gummy bears. On days that I spent an absurd amount of time in the bathroom, activated charcoal came to the rescue, but it was only a quick fix, not a cure. I might as well have flushed the lactose intolerance pills and histamine blockers directly down the toilet. I popped vitamins because the purple chewables I ate as a child cured everything, as did my vitamin fortified Sugar Puffs. I often wonder whether the processed foods I consumed while growing up may have contributed to my colon cancer. Fresh ingredients were old-fashioned in the sixties. Tasty, empty calories courtesy of the Industrial Food Revolution were hip.

My desperate search continued for nearly a year. Then, one day, I stumbled across probiotic bacteria. Their performance has been spectacular, and my gut has rewarded me with predictability. Not only that, those linebackers have prevented me from getting a cold and restored my dry, cracked hands to a pleasantly smooth state. A few times a week, I stir seven billion bacilli into a glass of water and gulp them down.

Approximately five pounds of bacteria, known as the microbiome, reside in our guts and significantly impact our lives. These beloved pets adore fiber and fermented foods, so feed them well. In fact, the large intestine handles more than digestion. It contains over one hundred million neurons and is often called the second brain. Ultimately, the brain and gut work in tandem and are a formidable team.

Avoiding a colonoscopy is like riding a motorcycle without a helmet. Get the test. Do you really want to be the one thinning out the population?

Dog School

When the newest member of our family was five months old, we enrolled him in dog school. The course was taught by two women, one of whom resembled a German Shepherd and was clearly the alpha female. Her confident demeanor implied that even the smallest ball of fluff would benefit from her superior canine wisdom. Under her tutelage, we, too, could become alphas. In terms of interspecies cohabitation, this woman understood dog-parenting inadequacies and warned us that a pet indifferent to human authority could ruin your life, your carpeting, and your shoes.

Dog school was a family affair, and I attended the classes with my husband and son. On the first day, the assistant handed out clickers and high-pitched training whistles. Then, the German Shepherd took over. "We'll begin with clicker training," she said authoritatively.

I raised my hand. "Excuse me, I have a question. At home, we speak German and English. Can we use either language here?"

"The commands are in German, but you can read him a bedtime story in English," she barked. "I hope everyone brought cheese."

Our first assignment was to give a cheese cube to our dog while clicking the clicker. Food is a mighty incentive, and Beethoven exhibited an unprecedented zeal for learning.

"Now I want you to guide your dog's derriere to the ground, command him to sit and stay, and reward him with cheese and a click."

It didn't take long for our furry prodigy to master sitting. But weren't we merely rewarding him for a trait he already had? Even so, we practiced sit, stay, click, and cheese to strengthen his infantile synapses.

I'd like to mention that the King Charles Spaniel ranks forty-fourth on the *Smartest Dog Breeds* list. Admittedly, our pet was not nimble-witted, but he far surpassed us regarding displays of affection. His 'I'm elated to see you' ballet was an unparalleled tour de force of adoration. In fact, it was soul-stirring to witness his profound happiness whenever we walked through the door.

Next on the syllabus was the art of lying down and staying. Yet again, we captured our dog's attention by holding a bit of cheese in front of his nose, which gave him considerable olfactory pleasure and reminded me of a sommelier scrutinizing the scent of a fine wine. The lesson began with our dog in a seated position. Slowly, we moved the treat toward the ground, and Beethoven earnestly followed the food, then lay down on the grass and stretched his hind legs behind him as if he were sunbathing. Our vigorous applause and a chorus of "Good dog, good boy!" accompanied his accomplishment. Following a brief pause, we bellowed, "Okay," and our clever pet tottered to his feet and wolfed down the treat. Remarkably, this skill provided us with the long awaited off-switch. Never again would the wound-up animal pirouette around our legs while we put on our shoes.

Join me as I explore the secret powers of the whistle, audible for half a mile to animals and humans alike. Get ready to become a canine wizard!

I slipped the whistle necklace over my head and cooed, sit, while backing away with my arm stretched and palm raised. After thirty paces, I raised the whistle to my lips and blew a short toot, followed by a long toot. Lo and behold, the dog raced toward me, and I greeted him with aged cheddar and a click. The whistle freed us from frantically shouting, "Come, boy, come here!" Which, I might add, he often ignored. Now, every time we entered the woods and released our pet from his leash, he rushed into our arms the moment we blew the whistle, even when he was completely distracted by the eu de toilette of his bucolic surroundings. If you own a dog but do not own a dog whistle, you lack the most crucial dog-owner accessory.

On the last day of class, dog school featured an obstacle course for athletic bow wows. The clueless dogs in our group meandered around the course, oblivious to the frustrated Border Collie observing them. The collie sat facing a row of poles, known as weave poles, well aware that he was the fastest, most agile, and intellectually gifted animal on the field. Beethoven sniffed, then clumsily squeezed through a couple of poles, causing the precocious observer tangible anguish. He was a sprinter waiting to bolt, and his wound-up body radiated an irrepressible force.

An invisible trainer blew a whistle, and the collie raced through the poles like a sewing machine making a zigzag stitch. A split second is all it took. His instantaneous speed and fluidity of movement were stunning. Beethoven sniffed a dandelion, unaware of the spectacular feat beside him. The Border Collie grabbed his book and retreated to a quiet corner of the field.

Did we envy the Border Collie owners? No, we did not. Border Collies, like ambitious people, require constant stimulation. They are restless and easily bored. I surely did not want to spend my days trying to satisfy an animal's intellectual and athletic needs. However, our dog's ancestors were busy keeping the aristocracy's laps warm. A Border Collie could not sit still long enough to keep anyone's lap from freezing and would never have the patience to pose for a portrait. Since the sixteenth century, artists such as Van Dyck, Stubbs, and countless others have depicted King Charles Cavalier Spaniels, dogs bred to be cuddly, sweet-tempered, affectionate, and downright adorable. Mary Queen of Scots even hid a small spaniel in the folds of her skirt to comfort her during her execution. Although, in that situation, a Rottweiler might have been the better choice. Queen Victoria's King Charles Spaniel, Dash, who, by the way, is the spitting image of our dog Beethoven, was preserved on canvas by the painter Sir Edwin Landseer and never had to suffer the trauma of his owner's demise.

Our dog was not endowed with the necessary gray matter to reach a higher rating on the intelligence list, and he would never shield us from harm if called to serve. Yet he could sit, stay, and come when summoned. And since we do not own sheep that require herding but occasionally have cold laps, we have everything we need.

Not So New Jersey

The New Jersey apartment I shared with the man I eventually married was a far cry from the pink carpeting and floral wallpaper of my childhood home. If anything, it brought to mind lodgings inhabited by starving Impressionists. Our bedroom boasted an air mattress flanked by cardboard boxes, and antlers my boyfriend Key found while hiking in a national park hung above our heads. We were lucky they didn't fall from the crumbling plaster wall at night and blind us. But, oh, what a focal point, an actual piece of artwork. Who needs decorative pillows or smoky bedside lighting when you have the ultimate representation of male virility jutting from a disembodied buck above your bed.

The day we moved in, we found a shrunken rat carcass on the closet floor. But the actual bohème moment occurred around midnight when a mouse scurried across my foot as I stumbled to the bathroom. It was so authentically bohemian that we joked about laughing at it one day. "Look at it this way," I groaned, "mice eat cockroaches, which makes them enemies with benefits. Besides, shouldn't couples enjoy the patter of little feet around the house?"

In terms of uninvited guests, it could have been worse. I once read an article about a New Orleans couple who turned a deaf ear to the termites devouring their home. We followed suit and ignored the silverfish, roaches, and mice frolicking inside our walls and traipsing in and out of gaps between the floorboards. Nevertheless, sleeping directly on the floor left us vulnerable to an unwanted threesome and put only six inches between our lungs and decades' worth of dust. Indeed, there is a vast difference between what I endured then and what I can tolerate today.

Not surprisingly, the stench of neglect spilled from the stairwell into our apartment until I replaced it with lime-scented cleaner and baked chicken. Back then, I wasn't roasting free-roaming poultry. We ate birds that hobbled in filth, had porn-sized breasts, and cost a buck fifty each. After using the oven for the first time, I forgot to remove the leftovers, and the following morning, I opened the oven door to a haughty Jersey mouse sitting in the pan, chewing on a chicken bone. My theatrical yelp didn't stop him from eating or waving his middle toe at me.

Some of our building's more memorable residents included a hunched-back, greasy-haired older man sporting an eye patch and a sullen woman who never reciprocated our neighborly nods. And yet, she was not opposed to us saving her life. Shortly after we moved in, we heard frantic pounding on our door. Despite my trepidation, I opened it, and there she stood, the unsociable woman struggling to breathe. Key sprang into action and performed the Heimlich maneuver. It took a few squeezes for him to dislodge the food, and you'd think she might have acknowledged this deed with a word or a gesture of appreciation, but she didn't. Once she began breathing normally, she shuffled away in silence. At least she wasn't feigning friendship, and honestly, skipping the empty small talk was a relief.

I must admit, seeing him rescue that woman was like watching a male bird of paradise dance his courtship tableau. My man may not have provided the best nest, but he could save a life. As a matter of fact, it was impressive enough to convince me that moving to New Jersey was the right decision. Although, the day we were out for a stroll and witnessed a man being held at gunpoint was not part of my counterculturist libretto.

What brought us to New Brunswick? Key decided to study with a violin professor at Rutgers University. This is what classical musicians do; they travel great distances, live in squalor, and pay the equivalent of ten hours of waitressing to a prominent musician who will provide the elixir vitae for winning an audition. Since my boyfriend's money ended up in his teacher's bank account, he cut back on the one thing he didn't care about, clothes. Baggy jeans and a stack of T-shirts featuring the words *Next One*, which he got for free at a car dealership's promotional event, belonged to his fashionless statement. Our lack of funds was also why we lived in a dilapidated hovel with a menagerie of non-human room-mates. We were seduced by the bliss of love, and the fiasco of our apartment, the financial crunch, and the mice only galvanized our amour.

Our romance began at the Tanglewood Music Festival the year before. From my perch in the clarinet section, I had a clear view of an exotic-looking violinist with a head of ink-black hair and chiseled good looks. He intrigued me, and every day during rehearsal, I wondered whether he was Indian, Asian, or possibly Mexican. One thing was certain: he was an extraordinary mix. Since I was too shy to approach him, I indulged in a one-sided, intensely romantic cerebral relationship instead.

Several weeks into the festival, Leonard Bernstein ar-rived to conduct Stravinsky's primal and emotionally charged *The Rite of Spring*. Lenny, as everyone called him, showed up to rehearsals wearing jeans and cowboy boots and treated us to a witty repartee before beginning. As he conducted, his genius unfolded with each wave of the baton and unleashed our passion. We were compelled to please him, and our unwavering adoration fueled the mu-sic.

Bernstein was a charismatic yet profound conductor who was as sophisticated as he was tempestuous, and the perfor-mance erupted like a volcano. After the concert, he hosted an equally fiery party. Music thumped in the overcrowded room, and a throbbing, collective abandon took hold. But I have misophonia and couldn't tolerate the fireworks, so I stepped outside. A moment later, the mysterious violinist joined me.

"I can't handle the noise," I said casually.

"Neither can I."

"I've been wondering where you're from?"

"Germany, but my mother is Japanese."

"Do you want to go for a walk?"

It's unimaginable to think that more than half of my life has been governed by this moment. Our paths would not have crossed had either of us left the party seconds earlier or later.

While living in New Brunswick, I practiced clarinet in the morning and worked afternoons at a library that smelled as fetid as our apartment building. The pleasantly dusty scent of old books may have been discernible to a German Shepherd, but was undeniably conquered by the pungent smell of ripe bodies lounging in the stacks.

Our neighborhood had an aura of decay. At least the streets weren't littered with abandoned shopping carts like the Chicago suburb where I accidentally ended up one morning. I was riding the 'L' and disembarked at the wrong stop. After leaving the station, I entered a dystopian world of shattered lives and buildings. Garbage littered the streets, and broken windows were boarded up with plywood. Desolate pets and people slept where they fell. While wandering the road opposite the station, a man approached me and said, "Turn around now and get back on that train."

We will never know how often a split-second decision was a life or death choice.

In another instance, I was waiting for a late-night train in Italy when an attractive man offered me a ride. I was twenty-one, naïve, and almost accepted. Fortunately, the man standing behind my future assailant shook his finger, warning me not to get into that car.

One day, brown sludge oozed from our drains and filled the sink and tub. Our bathroom looked like a septic tank; however, using a plunger was out of the question. To begin with, I knew it wouldn't work, and we'd probably end up covered in toxic dreck. Besides, if that happened, where were we supposed to wash it off? We could not have caused a clog of this magnitude in such a short time. Maybe mice wedged themselves into the pipes, I mused. In any case, it seemed unlikely that creatures using squeaks and chirps to communicate could have coordinated a simultaneous sink and tub occupation. Did you know that mice can sing, supposedly like birds, but you can't hear them. I won't be convinced until I can stream their songs on Spotify.

In the end, we called the superintendent, who arrived later that day with a snake. Not only were we shocked to discover that the hunched-back man was our custodian, but up close, he was clearly in his mid-thirties and not elderly.

Our New Jersey odyssey lasted three months, while our relationship has flourished for thirty-six years. We tied the knot because we were in love. However, we stayed married because we fit together like puzzle pieces. Our differences compensate for each other's shortcomings, yet as pieces of the same puzzle, we take pleasure in our similarities. At the end of the day, the salt in our soupe du jour is humor, which makes life delicious despite the occasional mouse frolicking in the bowl.

Schadenfreude

Schadenfreude is a German word that expresses the satisfaction we get from the misfortune of others. The emotion is visceral and wedged somewhere between feigned pity and gratification. It's difficult to find an English equivalent; furtive gloating doesn't quite smack you in the face like schadenfreude. I've always been fascinated by the word's candor. People rarely admit to experiencing schadenfreude. This live-wire word hovers behind a facade of commiseration. Nevertheless, schadenfreude is embedded in our brains and in lexicons around the globe. Can I interest you in a croissant and a little *joie maliceuse*, or would you prefer *gioia maliziosa* with your espresso?

Years ago, the equine magic that often strikes young girls lured my daughter to horse camp. Was this a budding passion or a whim? I had no idea, but it was impossible to resist her doe eyes, so I made plans for her to attend the weeklong program. Since a friend of hers was also going, they decided to share a room.

Before heading off to horse country, we spent a decent amount of money on equestrian paraphernalia and pricey breeches, known as jodhpurs. We packed it all up a few weeks later and drove to camp. Considering the drive took only twenty minutes, it was really an outing on training wheels.

As we wandered the grounds searching for the office, a high school student in sleek riding boots led us to a run-down building. We didn't expect the equestrian Hilton, but this place had passed its sell-by date. Alas, during registration, we discovered that our daughter's chum had chosen a new roommate, and our child would have to share a room with a stranger. You can't take away your kid's pain, but you can turn the predicament into an enriching experience and a horizon broadening event.

"Look at it this way," I said with a forced smile, "you're going to make a new friend."

My daughter rolled her eyes.

Approximately a week after camp ended, the mother of her intended roommate called to inquire whether my child got lice during her stay.

"No, my daughter didn't get lice, did yours?"

"She did, and it was horrible. The whole room was infested."

Well, the schadenfreude genie was out of the bottle and would take a romp around the therapeutic feeling of retribution.

Lice are a messy business. Their eggs, called nits, nestle in your child's scalp, and baby lice, dubbed nymphs, frolic in the forest of hair. You get rid of these parasitic insects by raking them away with a fine-toothed comb and then vigorously scrubbing your offspring's scalp with an expensive medicated shampoo. The truth is, your efforts do not guarantee the death of the pests. Bedding and clothing must be soaked, agitated, and spun in the hottest water your washing machine can provide. Small stuffed animals are sent away for a vacation in the freezer. My freezer barely has room for a louse, let alone the object it calls home. The oversized teddy bear Aunt Lolly gave your kid for Christmas must be suffocated in a plastic bag for two weeks.

Does the feeling of schadenfreude reveal human weakness? Of course it does. Whatever emotions we experience during our gloating session, the triumph of justice legitimatizes them. Given that schadenfreude is a harsh word, we'll sprinkle it with sugar; you're simply unsympathetic to someone else's predicament.

Often, the success of others and their material possessions trigger schadenfreude. The same goes for games. Does a child feel brotherly love when his sibling wins a giant panda playing ring toss at the church carnival? Maybe, but the relationship has become somewhat lopsided, even if the winner is not flaunting their victory. Sometimes, we feel cheated out of something we didn't even want.

I could be writing this in cuneiform on a clay tablet, and schadenfreude would rear its ugly head. You had a big yam harvest, and I didn't. Then, one night, a rat ate your yams and knocked the chip off my shoulder with its last bite.

I'd never bet on a game, but I'd wager that schadenfreude has a box seat at the stadium despite wearing a friendly rivalry T-shirt.

Life is a veritable fiesta of mishaps and embarrassing moments, and there are times when we are comforted by the blunders of others. Instead of lamenting a problem, schadenfreude allows us to deflect it. We're not necessarily reveling in another person's dilemma, but merely diluting our own despair.

You know, I think I'll open a bottle of wine and ponder the advice of Marcus Aurelius to dwell on the beauty of life.

About the Author

Kim Märkl, born in Cleveland, is an author, composer, and clarinetist. Her stories and music have been featured in audiobooks, and performances of her works, including two plays, have taken place throughout Europe. She is the founder of Atlantic Crossing Records, a label known for its unique fusion of words and music. After receiving a Fulbright Grant, she settled in Germany, where she lives with her husband and two children. *I Can't Wear Wool* is her debut book of essays.